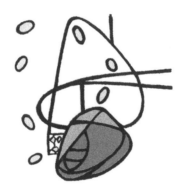

The Life, Times and Work of
CHARLES RENNIE MACKINTOSH

K. E. Sullivan

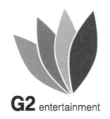

G2 entertainment

For Melanie, a friend indeed

Acknowledgements

The author would like to thank Lucinda Hawksley, Sonya Newland, Frances Banfield and Nick Wells at the Foundry, for their support and encouragement. I am indebted to the Charles rennie Mackintosh Society, the Glasgow School of Art and the Hunterian Art Gallery, all of whom provided help and advice. I would also like to acknowledge Allan Crawford's *Charles Rennie Mackintosh*, which presented a comprehensive and unbiased picture of the man and his work. Quotations from that book are reprinted with permission of his publishers, Thames & Hudson, London.

The Charles Rennie Mackintosh Society is based in Queen's Cross Church, 870 Garscube Road, Glasgow G20 7EL.

Also Grateful thanks to Helen Courtney for her work on this project.

First published in 1997 by Brockhampton Press
an Imprint of The Caxton Publishing Group

ISBN: 978-1-78281-998-1

Contents

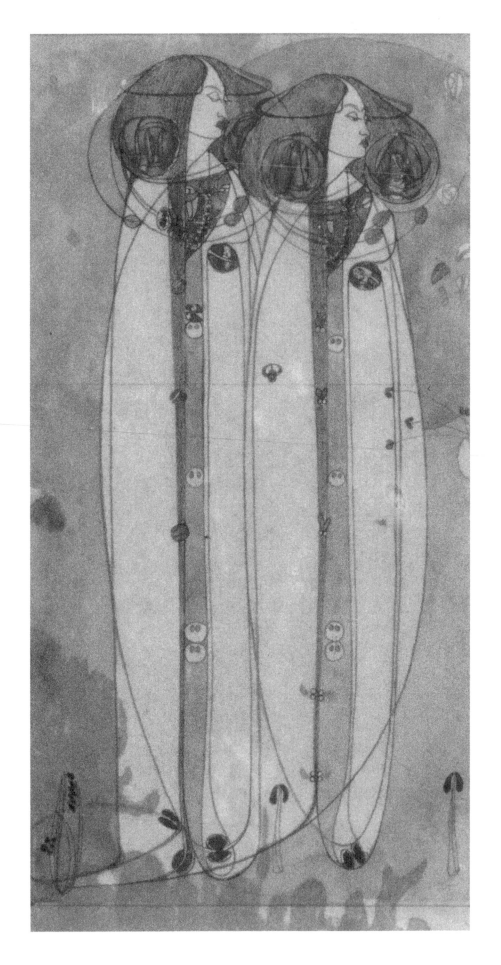

CHARLES RENNIE MACKINTOSH

INTRODUCTION

*Every object which you pass from your hand must carry an outspoken
mark of individuality, beauty and most exact execution.*

Charles Rennie Mackintosh, 1902

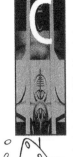 HARLES RENNIE MACKINTOSH is recognized as one of the most
important and original designers of the twentieth century, considered
by many to be a forerunner of the Modern Movement and Art Deco.
He was a man of courageous vision who spent his life in the search of
perfection, mastering the decorative arts, architecture, design and
painting with a determination matched only by his intense self-belief.
His work reflected the cool, clear thinking of a man who could form a
coherent and comprehensive ideology and spend the most part of his
life in its pursuit.

Mackintosh was an avid theorist: he adopted and adapted the
doctrines of some of the great figures of his time to fulfil his own
ambition and desire for a holistic approach to art. He was both unique
and challenging, and although his work was never sufficiently recognized
in his day, some of his greatest achievements have now become icons,
as relevant today as they were a century ago.

He was an uncompromising man, with an uncompromising style,
and in his most productive years he created a world of aesthetic
sensibility. Since his death he has been lauded as both a pioneer and
canon of his age, and his remarkable, sophisticated and unique *oeuvre* is
celebrated worldwide.

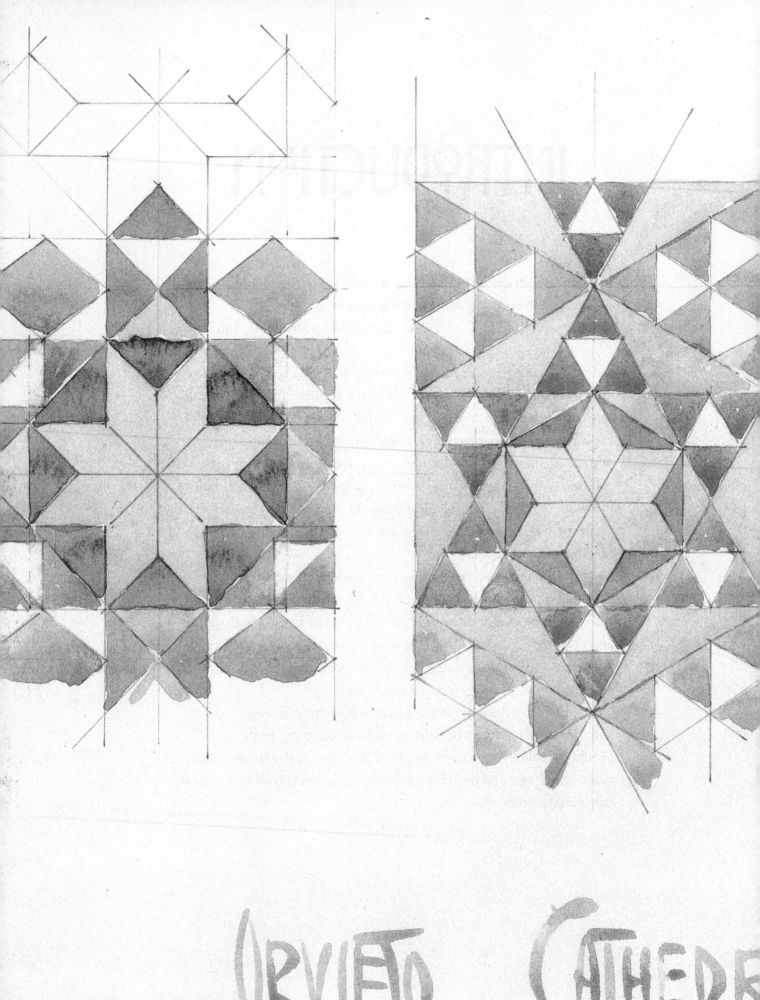

ORVIETO CATHEDR

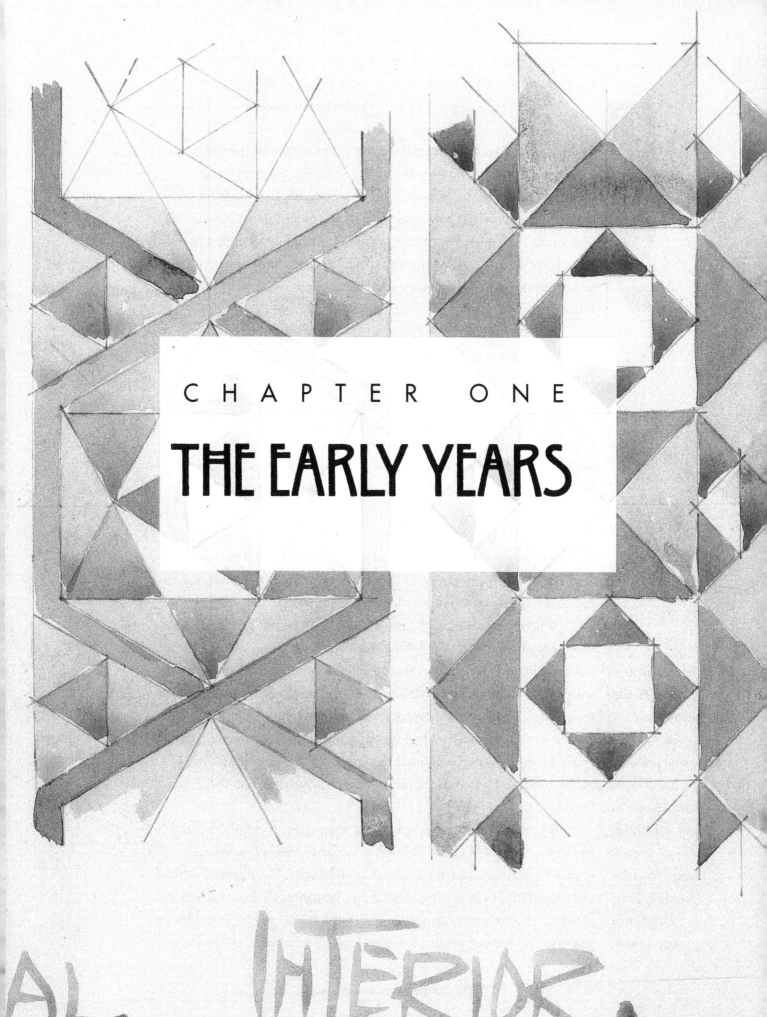

CHAPTER ONE
THE EARLY YEARS

... my pride is in ... the architecture of our own country, just as much Scotch as we are ourselves.

Charles Rennie Mackintosh, 1893

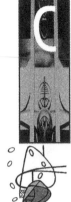

harles Rennie Mackintosh was born on 7 June 1868, in the oldest part of Glasgow. His first home was 70 Parson Street, a tenement like countless others in the area, and like their neighbours, his family was working class. Charles was the fourth of eleven children, but the flat was larger than most tenements, although probably cramped by modern standards, and it accommodated the family comfortably. As a result, Mackintosh's early years were happy ones, marked by order and a close family environment rather than by poverty.

His father, William McIntosh, was a superintendent in the Glasgow Police, a good, respectable position, and he took great pride in raising a virtuous, Presbyterian family. He was a strict father, unsympathetic to flights of fancy and imagination, but his Highland roots had given him a passion for gardening, and he instilled in young Charles a profound knowledge of and intimacy with nature. His mother, born Margaret Rennie, was a warm, energetic woman, and their house was filled with fresh flowers and spirited discourse.

Mackintosh was not robust. He was born with a contracted sinew in one foot which caused him to limp, a drooping eyelid, and a form of dyslexia which made his schooling difficult. His doctor advised plenty of exercise, and he took great delight in wandering the lush countryside surrounding the city.

When he was six, his family moved to 2 Firpark Terrace, a new tenement in Dennistoun, a prospering, middle-class suburb. Their flat was considerably larger than their previous home and in comparison with their neighbours, the McIntoshes lived in some affluence. He spent many of his years at Dennistoun working with his father in the garden of a neighbouring abandoned house, which became his playground. He spent many hours there, experiencing nature first-hand and imbibing a love of the natural world that would remain with him for the rest of his life.

When he was seven, Mackintosh went to Reid's Public School, and at nine, to Allan Glen's School in Cathedral Street, a private school for the children of tradesmen and artisans. His physical difficulties caused him to take little pleasure in the games of the local school children, and he spent many hours wandering the countryside. His instincts and love of nature, combined with an exquisite talent for

Glass Detail from Hill House.
Recurring themes and motifs are found throughout Mackintosh's interiors: stencilled on the wallpaper; as insets in the furniture; in the fireplace surrounds or the light fittings. These motifs often took the form of flowers or other organic images.

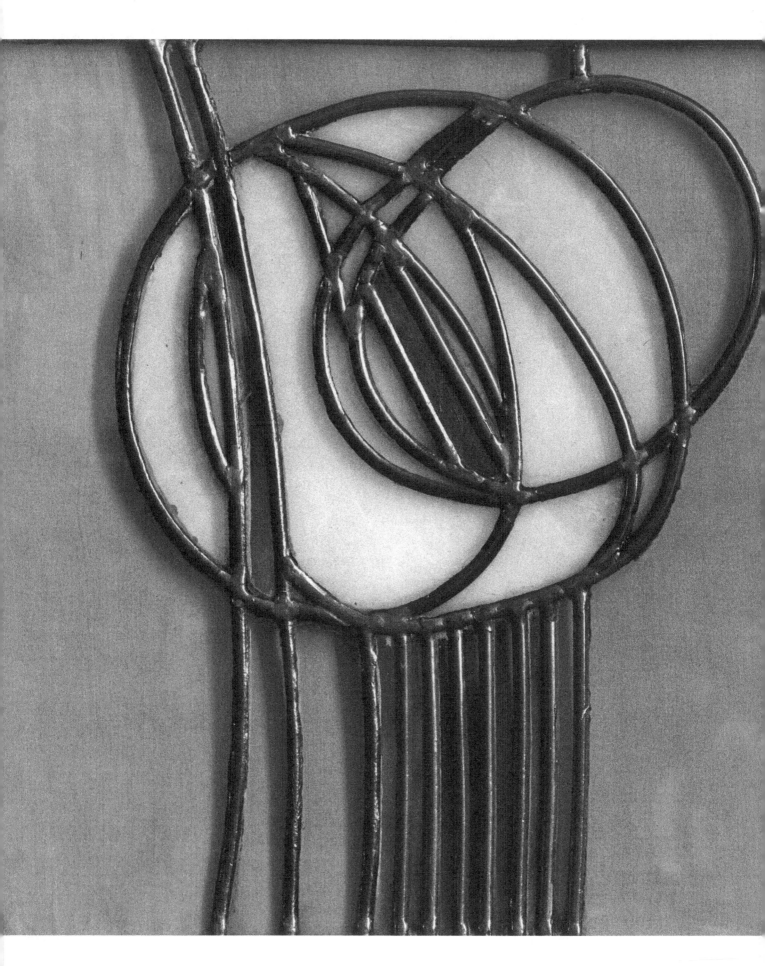

THE EARLY YEARS

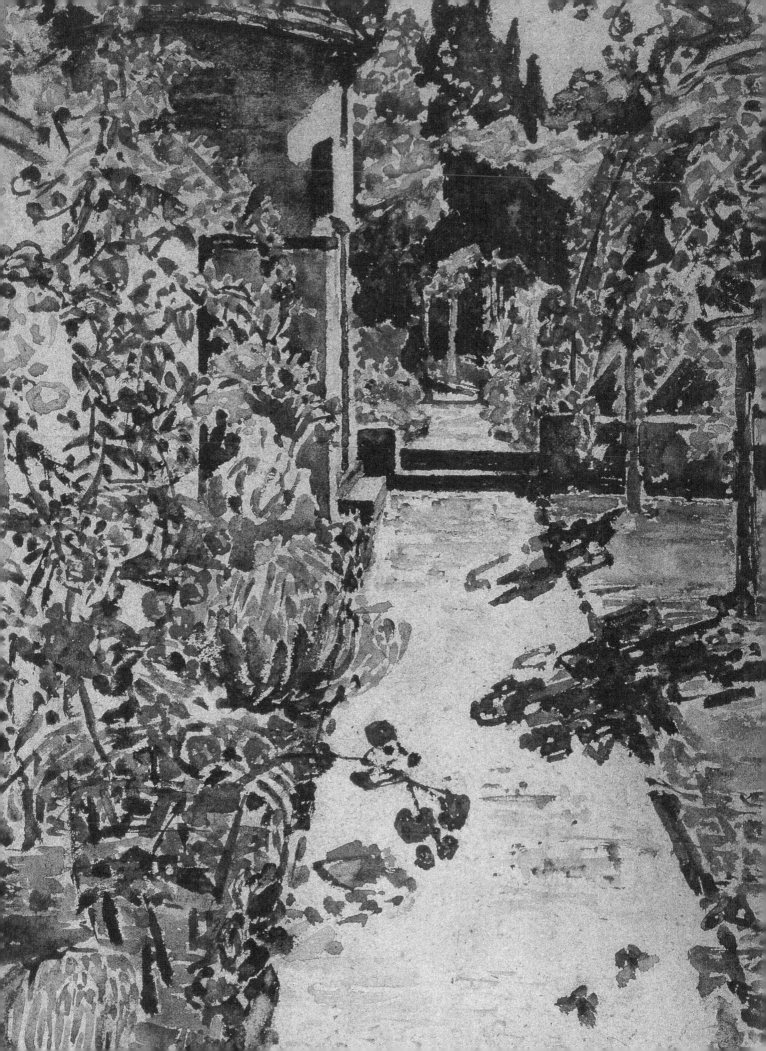

sketching, encouraged him to fill countless notebooks with nature studies and sketches of the buildings he encountered. The fusion of these two passions sowed the seeds of his later work, which amalgamated structure and nature in one holistic entity.

Mackintosh grew strong with his wanderings, and he became well-known locally for his cheerful personality and considerable talents. His father had brought up his children to be strong, independent individuals, and it was with characteristic determination that Mackintosh announced, at the age of fifteen, that he wished to become an architect, and enrolled in the Glasgow School of Art. A year later, he was articled to the little-known architectural practice of John Hutchison. He attended the School of Art in the early mornings and evenings, spending his days in the small offices of Hutchison's practice.

In the late nineteenth century, architects were trained in the offices of their employers and only the most ambitious young men studied art to improve their skills. Mackintosh was one of these, keen to make use of his talents, he worked hard at art school, winning numerous prizes for his 'care and fidelity'. At the time, the Glasgow School of Art was known for the rigorous training it offered young men and women of talent and according to the school itself, they were expected to 'give themselves

THESE TWO PASSIONS SOWED THE SEEDS OF HIS LATER WORK

body and soul to their work and to submit to a rigid curriculum and course of study', particularly that of antique and historic sources. They studied a variety of disciplines, intended to give them a solid background in all manner of arts and techniques. In 1885, Francis Newbery became headmaster of the Glasgow School of Art. He was a brilliant man under whom the school flourished and he fostered in the students a great pride in their unique creativity. Newbery was a firm believer in the importance of modern movements, in particular the Arts and Crafts movement, the Japanese arts, which were beginning to influence art and design in Scotland, and the decorative arts.

Mackintosh's formal training in architecture did not begin until 1886, giving him his first opportunity to hone the skills that he had been using on a day-to-day basis in the offices of John Hutchison. In 1889, at the age of 24, he completed his apprenticeship and joined the newly formed architectural firm of Honeyman and Keppie. John Honeyman was the senior partner of the establishment, and at fifty-eight

The Garden at Hill House, Helensburgh.
Mackintosh acquired a love of nature in childhood, and as he grew older, this passion was reflected in much of his work — in his painting, textiles and designs.

he had a distinguished record. He had, however, suffered a few business problems and in 1888, in order to give the firm a new lease of life, he took on a new partner, John Keppie. Keppie was twenty-seven, educated and wealthy, and his sophisticated taste and efficient administration of the business attracted a new clientele for the company, transforming it into one of the most important and lucrative in Glasgow.

Mackintosh began at Honeyman and Keppie as a draftsman, but his exceptional abilities were soon recognized, and he joined forces with Keppie on many early occasions. The junior partner enjoyed both the talents and the character of the young draftsman, who was cheerful, confident and amusingly arrogant in his opinions.

In the nineteenth century, Glasgow's architecture was both comprehensive and uniform, built almost entirely of stone and drawing on Classical traditions such as that of nearby Edinburgh. While other cities began to diversify and draw on other schools of design, Glasgow retained her haughty conformity to the distinguished styles that had been her more recent heritage. Partly responsible for this slavish devotion to the Classicist ideology was Alexander 'Greek' Thomson, who invested the tradition with inspiring revivals of styles from Ancient Egypt, Rome, the Renaissance, the Gothic era, Medieval times and, in particular, Greek sources. It was said that when Thomson died in 1875, the Classical tradition almost died with him, and Mackintosh's early years in the architectural practice were witness to exciting new trends in design that began slowly to make themselves known.

Mackintosh's architectural training at the Glasgow School of Art and at both offices gave him good practical experience combined with essential theory, and his imaginative approach made him a popular member of the Honeyman and Keppie practice. In 1890 Mackintosh won the coveted 'Alexander Thomson Travelling Studentship' for his *Public Hall* design, which, with its colonnaded front, drew on early Classical traditions. With his prize of £60 he decided to make an extensive tour of Italy, via Paris, Brussels, Antwerp and London.

Shortly before his departure, Mackintosh was invited to read a paper at the Glasgow Architectural Association, an indication of his growing recognition in the architectural world. He chose 'Scotch Baronial Architecture' as his subject, and the lecture has remained an oft-discussed landmark in his career. Mackintosh stressed the importance of tradition in architecture, expressing a wish that his own and future generations would look to the roots of Scots architecture and 'make the style conform to modern requirements'. A style that

Flower Study in Pencil and Watercolour.
Throughout his lifetime, Mackintosh travelled widely in Britain and in Europe where he spent much of his time sketching elements of his two main interests — nature and architecture.

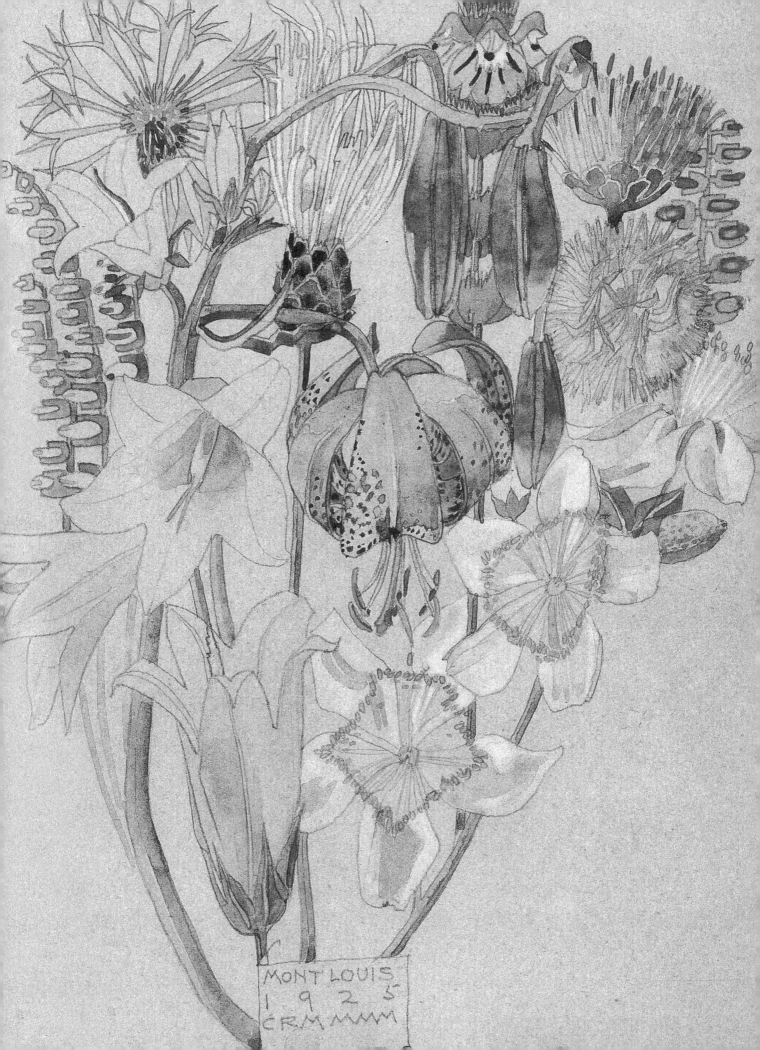

MONT LOUIS
1925
CRMMM

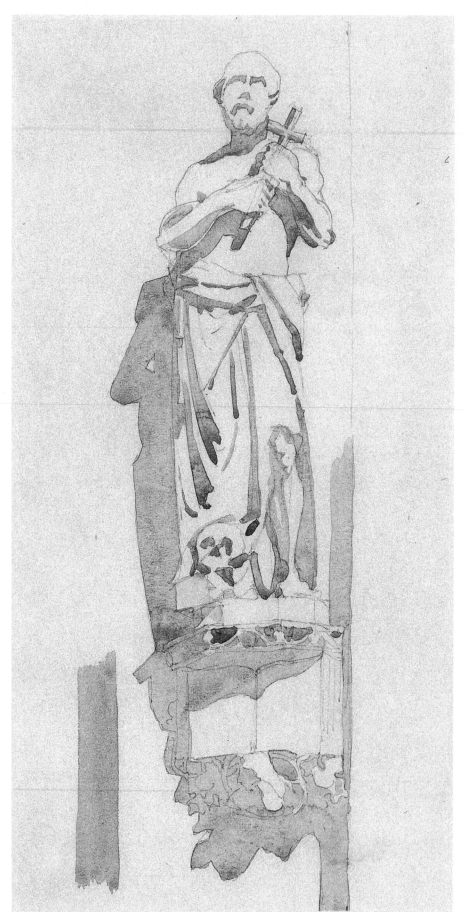

Study of a Statue of
St Jerome, Milan
Cathedral.
*While journeying through
Italy, Mackintosh was
impressed by the archi-
tecture and details of the
cathedrals and churches,
and he sketched many points
of interest, including
statues, columns, windows
and mosaics.*

would forge links with the past, but not be bound by it.

On 21 March 1891, Charles left Glasgow for his three-month sketching tour of Europe. In this time, he filled notebook after notebook with churches, museums, mosaics, libraries, benches and windows. He took copious notes on things he admired, and sketched exquisitely detailed drawings of ornaments, features, hinges and all manner of detail and decoration. He was thrilled by the early styles of the Romanesque, Gothic and Byzantine, rather than the classic architecture of the Renaissance, and explored cities and small villages alike, combing them for intriguing combinations of architectural aspects. His preferences mirrored those of many of his contemporaries, including John Dand Sedding, George Frederick Bodley and Henry Wilson, all of whose work exerted a significant influence on Mackintosh's own. His notebooks point to his expanding repertoire of organic and vernacular forms through sketches, watercolours and craftwork, and a selection from this body of work was subsequently awarded first prize in the Annual Exhibition of the School of Art Students' Club.

Mackintosh's pilgrimage to Italy undoubtedly opened his eyes to the dynamism of European architecture, and was a major formative influence on his development. The trip also set the seal on Mackintosh's professional status, and provided him with enormous confidence at the beginning of his career. Mackintosh's journey confirmed his beliefs rather than changing his views – unlike so many artists and architects before him, his work was not dramatically altered; he did not consider it a life-changing experience.

Charles had gone to Italy armed with a wealth of theory, having devoured the texts of artist and critic John Ruskin and the architect Augustus W. N. Pugin as part of his course-work. He began to form a concept of architecture which used the views of these men as a basis, one that was founded on the principle that historical styles were 'absurd', believing that the time was ripe for a 'new' language. He asserted that Scotland had a heritage which should be respected, and he held the great Scottish architects in high esteem – figures like James Sellars and John James Burnet were to be honoured and emulated. He drew inspiration from the more radical practitioners, such as William Richard Lethaby and C. F. A. Voysey, and keeping in mind Lethaby's statement that 'At the heart of ancient building there was wonder, magic and symbolism; the motive of our [buildings] must be human service, intelligible structure and verifiable science', Mackintosh was critical of many of the structures of Italy, commenting in particular

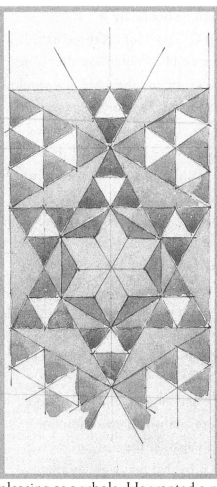

on the cathedral at Siena. He wrote: 'To begin with the whole front is a fraud as it gives no indication of the interior ... the design is almost not there.'

Mackintosh was struck by the magic of Southern Europe, and stood in awe at the majesty of her architecture, but he journeyed home with one thing in mind – that Scotland had her own architectural language, one which must be respected and modernized. He looked to England, he was to call upon Scotland's heritage, and then he looked further, for something that would allow him to profess the functional elegance of massive and towering Scotch buildings with the clean lines he knew were necessary to make it aesthetically pleasing as a whole. He wanted a new architecture without outside historical associations, one in which form and purpose were inextricably linked. He looked, then, to the Far East – to Japan in particular – which formed perhaps the greatest influence of Mackintosh's early years and wove a rich pattern throughout his work for the remainder of his career. And by drawing inspiration from so many sources and combining them to form a symbolic and highly individual design, Mackintosh developed his own style, the 'new' architecture of his vision.

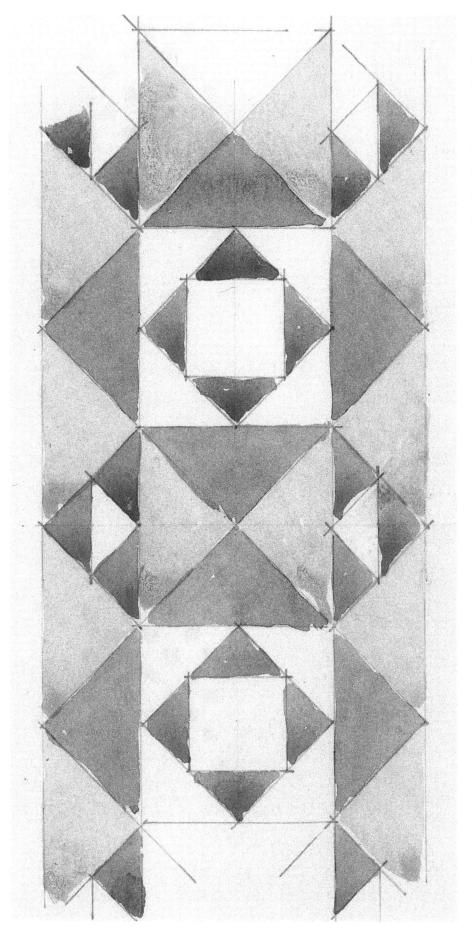

Mosaic Bands from a Cathedral Interior. *Mackintosh stayed at Orvieto in Italy in May 1891. He spent most of his time sketching the cathedral and its interior designs, which he thought 'most beautiful'.*

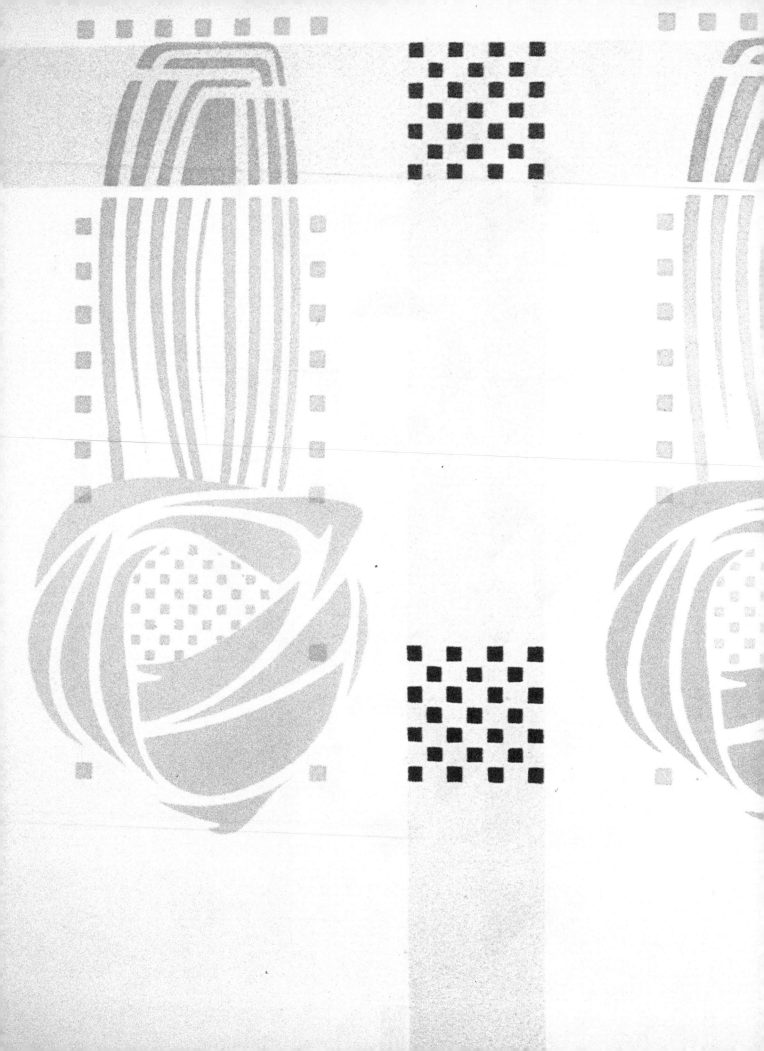

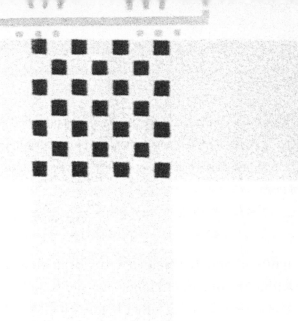

CHAPTER TWO

THE GLASGOW FOUR AND THE GLASGOW STYLE

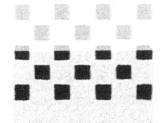

... But there is so much decorative method in his perversion of humanity that despite all the ridicule and abuse it has excited, it is possible to defend his treatment, for when a man has something to say and knows how to say it the conversion of others is usually but a question of time.

The Studio, 1897

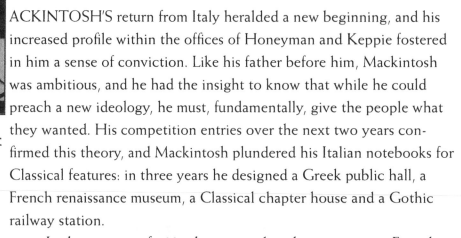

MACKINTOSH'S return from Italy heralded a new beginning, and his increased profile within the offices of Honeyman and Keppie fostered in him a sense of conviction. Like his father before him, Mackintosh was ambitious, and he had the insight to know that while he could preach a new ideology, he must, fundamentally, give the people what they wanted. His competition entries over the next two years confirmed this theory, and Mackintosh plundered his Italian notebooks for Classical features: in three years he designed a Greek public hall, a French renaissance museum, a Classical chapter house and a Gothic railway station.

In the summer of 1891, he returned to the tenement in Firpark Terrace. A year later his family moved to a terraced house in Regent Park Square, a symbol of their improved financial position. Mackintosh's mother had died in 1885 and his father had re-married to Christina Forrest, a widow. Although Mackintosh did not form a close relationship with the newly married couple, he continued to live with them. In 1895 the family moved to a new house in the same road, 27 Regent Park Square, and Mackintosh took up a room in the basement. Here, he had his first opportunity to express his artistic personality in his own home: the walls were papered and stencilled with a wide frieze of slender, undulating females with long, flowing hair and beneath that, stylized cats – the crest of the Mackintosh clan – under large suns and moons. He removed the new fireplace, left the old cottage grate with 3 plain surround, and hung Pre-Raphaelite and Japanese prints on his walls – an indication of his influences and interests at the time. He also produced a cabinet of his own design, simple and functional, yet visually appealing.

Throughout this time, his studies at the School of Art continued, and he formed a close friendship with fellow draughtsman Herbert MacNair, who was also employed at Honeyman and Keppie. The pair shared a vision of a new and symbolic architecture. Francis Newbery

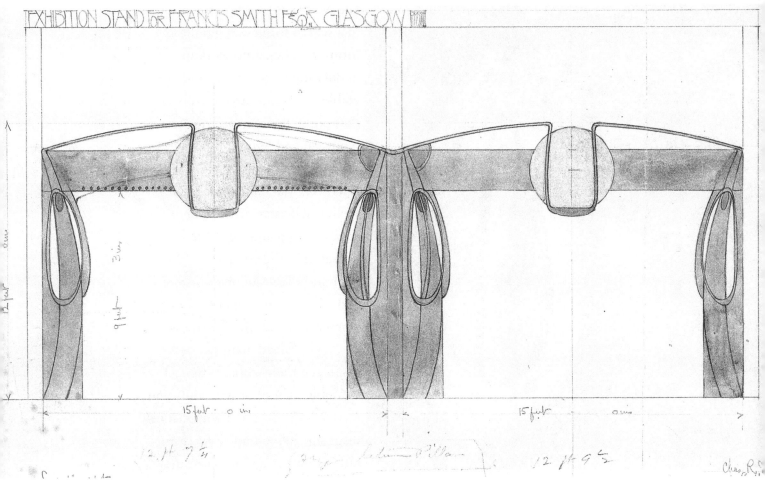

had by this time transformed the School, promoting the newest trends in art, design, craft and architecture. With Newbery keen to nurture the talents of the local artists and craftsmen, the atmosphere of the school was one of creative freedom rather than being traditionally and oppressively Victorian. In 1893, he introduced Mackintosh and MacNair to two young English sisters of Scottish descent – Frances and Margaret Macdonald, the daughters of an English solicitor, who had settled in Glasgow in the 1880s. The sisters had enrolled as day students at the school in 1891, in order to study painting. Margaret and Frances were described by Gleeson White in *The Studio*, as 'laughing, comely girls', and their artistic and romantic unions created the core of what would become the Glasgow Style. With characteristic brilliance, Newbery had noted the similarity between the approaches of the four artists, and he suggested that they collaborate to enhance their collective convictions.

The close, artistic relationship between the four was instantaneous, and they quickly became known for their easily identifiable style. Their interests were similar – based on a mutual talent and interest in poetry, the Celtic world, symbolism and mysticism. Mackintosh (Toshie)

Design for an Exhibition Stand.

The Glasgow Four exhibited their work on a number of occasions, where it was commonly met with criticism for its unusual structure, design and symbolism.

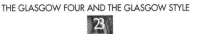

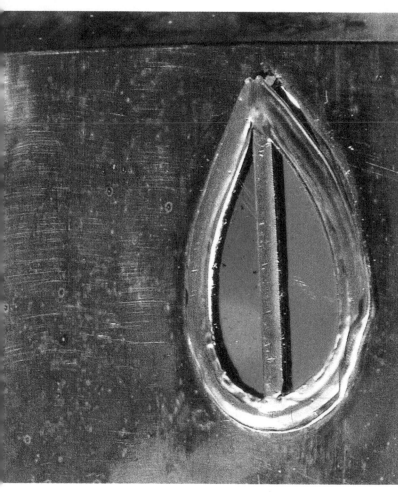

Detail of Metal and Leaded Glass Lampshade.

The Glasgow Style was adopted in the form of many materials. Previously, metal had been a relatively unknown artistic medium, but The Glasgow Four put it to effective creative use, perhaps most successfully in light fittings.

and MacNair (Bertie) joined forces in a search for new symbolic forms, and began to work in undulating lines, animal and vegetable forms and strong colours that pointed more towards Art Nouveau and Symbolism than their own native Arts and Crafts tradition. Mackintosh began to see himself as an artist rather than a young architect. He felt liberated in the company of Mac-Nair and the Macdonald sisters, and the feminine influences of the women were adopted with ease.

The Macdonald sisters displayed their work at the Glasgow School of Art exhibition in 1894, where it met with critical disparagement. 'Impossible forms, lurid colour and symbolism that requires many footnotes of explanation', 'Ghoul like', 'nightmare works' read the reviews, and the infamy soon led them to be called 'The Spook School', a name they cherished and in which they secretly revelled. Attention in any form was helpful for a young artist, and controversy served both to sell paintings and inspire critical debate. MacNair and Mackintosh were identified with Margaret and Frances, the shared notoriety confirming their belief in their ideology.

The Macdonald sisters painted thin, androgynous women, surrounded by stylized lines symbolizing tendrils of hair, or of plants. Their critics complained that their distortion was unhealthy, overtly feminist and painfully erotic. MacNair and Mackintosh admired them, understanding their symbolic meaning. MacNair later explained the nature of their integral symbolism: 'not a line was drawn without purpose, and rarely was a single motive employed that had not some allegorical meaning'.

Exhibiting together for the first time in Liège in 1895, The Glasgow Four produced works of mysterious symbolism and elegant, elongated lines. They drew their inspiration from the Pre-Raphaelite Brotherhood, a movement headed by poet and painter Dante Gabriel

Rossetti, who believed in a senti-
mental and nostalgic return to
medievalism. The Pre-Raphaelites
asserted that art had taken a wrong
turn three centuries earlier with
the formal influence of Raphael
and the Renaissance. Rebelling
against the excesses and abuses of
the art of the day, they determined
to drop the aesthetic styles of the
post-Raphael artists and bring
about a new moral seriousness.
The brotherhood strove to re-
discover the purity and nobility in
art and to adopt a naturalistic
approach, based on vivid colours
and exquisite detail. They aspired
to the honesty and simplicity of
primitive Christian artists – in particular, Lasinio's engravings of
fourteenth-century frescos in the

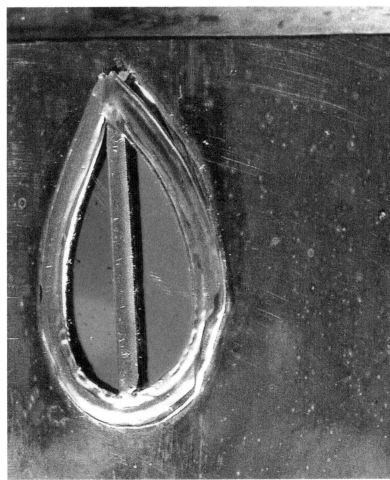

Campo Santo at Pisa – and they wanted to paint pictures, as Millais
wrote, that 'turned the minds of men to good reflections'. The Pre-
Raphaelites also believed whole-heartedly in the power of the imagination,
this was something with which The Glasgow Four could strongly
identify, imbuing their work with spiritual and symbolic significance.
Like the Pre-Raphaelites they determined to reject the conservatism
and materialism of the Victorian age.

The work of The Four was also influenced by the sinuous lines
of Aubrey Beardsley's illustrations in *The Yellow Book*, and they took
tremendous inspiration from Continental symbolism. They believed
that art should be organic, deriving from the 'melancholy and power
of nature', and were heavily influenced by Patrick Geddes' magazine
The Evergreen, which suggested links between the Celtic traditions of
Scotland's past and the present day.

Mackintosh began to use similar images to the Macdonalds –
tall, sensuous, elongated women, roses, trees, vines and round, fertile
moons and suns. But his work kept his own style, and he became synonymous with the infant Glasgow Style, and its diverse group of
themes. The Style was a loosely formed movement, but distinctive and

**Detail of Metal and
Leaded Glass
Lampshade.**

*Imagery of the natural
world was a characteristic
of The Four's designs – such
as the blue petal motif on
this lampshade. The idea of
a naturalistic approach to
art, and the vivid colours
they used, were inspired by
the Pre-Raphaelite movement.*

enthusiastic in its approach. Their themes were of mysticism and nature, with an overwhelming use of symbols: the rose, the dove, and the curiously distorted women that became their trademark. The Glasgow Style was adopted in many materials, including embroidery and stained glass, repoussé metalwork and copper, typography, furniture, textiles, ceramics, bookbinding and illustrations, and The Four were unquestionably the innovators of the approach. The movement attracted a group of women artists who adopted the feminine ideology, and their numbers included Janet Aitkin, Muriel Boyd, Helen Paxton Brown, Ailsa Craig, Mary and Margaret Gilmour, Jane Younger and Jessie Newbery, Francis Newbery's wife. They also included the male artists Peter Wylie Davidson. E. A. Taylor and George Walton.

Around the same time, there appeared a home-spun periodical called *The Magazine*, created and edited by Lucy Raeburn. This was circulated among the students, many of whom contributed water-colours, drawings or poetry, before passing it on to a fellow member of the student body. Over time, the magazine would be completed, and then recirculated. The first issue appeared in 1893, and The Glasgow Four contributed to all eleven issues over the next two years. Their personal style was considered to be lyrical and ethereal, con-trasting very pointedly and specifically to Scottish painting of the past, as represented by the Glasgow Boys. Mackintosh's images were less gloomy than the Macdonald sisters, and he focused on images of growth – roots, stems, branches and flowers, with vertical lines that curve and swoop in elegant motion. Each of The Four used stylized forms based on organic motifs, and interspersed them with humans, flowers, roses, butterflies aid peacocks. Mackintosh contributed *Cabbages in an Orchard*, the *Tree of Influence* and the *Tree of Personal Effort*, each of which had a unique message.

Following their watercolour work, The Four collaborated on poster designs which were both original and somewhat more appeal-ing to the masses. One of their strongest supporters was Gleeson White, editor of *The Studio* magazine, who wrote: '... it must never be forgotten that the purpose of a poster is to attract notice, and the mildest eccentricity would not be out of place provided it aroused curiosity and so riveted the attention of passers-by. Mr Mackintosh's posters may be somewhat trying to the average person .... But there is so much decorative method in his perversion of humanity that despite all the ridicule and abuse it has excited, it is possible to defend his treatment ...'.

Metal and Leaded Glass Hanging Shade. *Mackintosh mixed his artistic mediums, using glass for colour and light and metal for functionability and modernity. This stunning lampshade brings out the stark and complementary contrast of the two.*

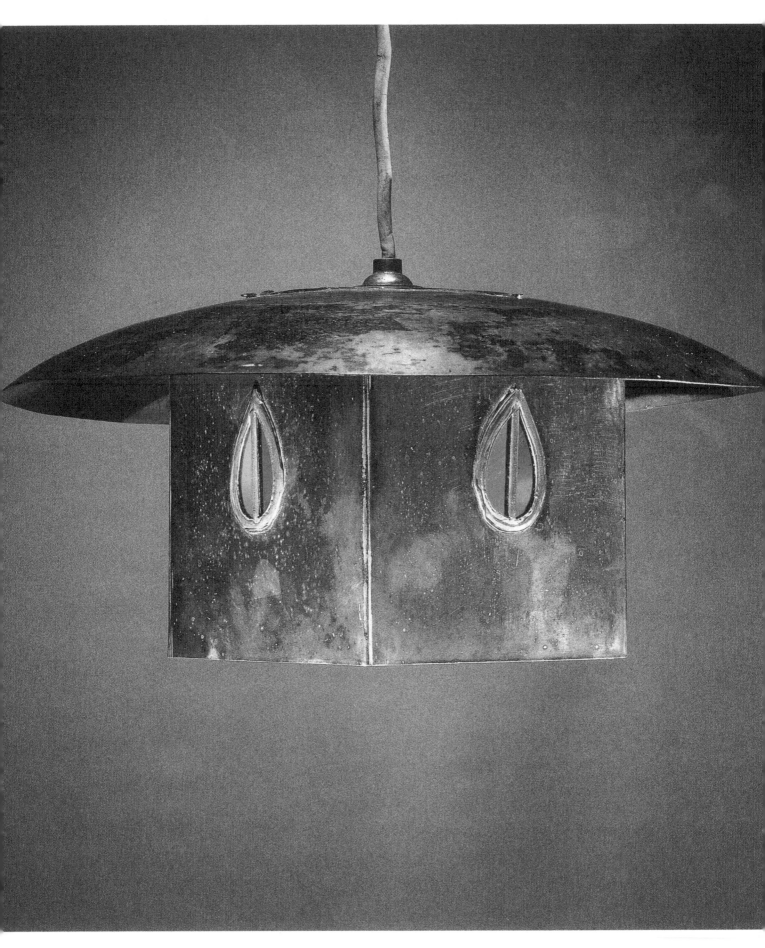

Their posters were controversial, but attention-grabbing. They were tall and narrow with decorative lettering and bold, mainly organic, stylized images, often employing the now characteristic motifs of lilies, roses and flying birds. In 1896, they produced posters for the Glasgow Institute of Fine Arts and *The Scottish Musical Review*, rich with severe and abstracted images that formed their heavily-styled decorative designs. Mackintosh in particular became known for his graphic art, and was commissioned to produce a number of murals and wall-stencils as a result.

Amid this blossoming of creativity the lives of The Four moved forward. The previous year, upon their graduation, the Macdonald sisters had opened up a studio. MacNair left Honeyman and Keppie to set up a private design practice on his own, specializing in craftwork and furniture design. Mackintosh continued in his lowly position at Honeyman and Keppie, with little actual building work to his credit, other than two semi-detached houses for his uncle William Hamilton, in 1890. In 1895 he rented a small studio where he worked on decorative commissions in his spare time.

MACKINTOSH'S FURNITURE DESIGN OF THIS PERIOD REFLECTS THE BURGEONING GLASGOW STYLE

Mackintosh had a number of commissions for murals, paintings and some furniture design, in particular for Guthrie and Wells, Glasgow furniture makers, for whom he created strong, robust pieces with a rich array of decorative detail that echoed his graphic work. Other commissions were made through friends or created specifically for exhibitions, but the studios of The Four had another purpose – that of informal meeting places for the artistic community of Glasgow, who were soon carrying the Glasgow Style into every arm of the arts.

Mackintosh's furniture design of this period reflects the burgeoning Glasgow Style. Wood was left unpainted, with clear varnishes and stains used to bring out the natural lustre and grain. Arts and Crafts and medieval themes were stencilled on furniture, or in leaded glass panels inserted into the wood. He used wide metal strap hinges, fusing age-old functionability with modern decoration. As yet most of his work took the form of one-off commissions, or suites of furniture, leaving Mackintosh no opportunity to prove his theory that architecture and interiors, furniture and furnishings, should form a holistic

Detail of a Wall Stencil from Hill House.

The images Mackintosh used in his work often reflected his love of nature, and the stylized rose motif is now one of the most familiar characteristics of his work.

unit. He continued to paint, draw, stencil and produce posters and furniture, but his architectural aspirations were clouded by his junior position within the firm. His relationship with Keppie also began to cool when Mackintosh ended his long-term romance with Keppie's sister Jessie, for Margaret Macdonald. As a result Keppie and Mackintosh's natural rapport was stifled. They did, however, work together on the remodelling of the Glasgow Art Club, and on alterations to the villa, Craigie Hall, including a new music room.

Detail of Mahogany Wash Stand.

The tree is a recurring theme throughout Mackintosh's design. Reflecting his fascination with the ancient Celtic cult of nature worship, he recreated this symbolism in the form of motifs incorporated into his furniture, his interiors – in particular the Willow Tearooms – and in his watercolours.

Despite these complications in his working life, Mackintosh's enthusiasms were satisfied by the frantic activity of The Four, who had generated interest in other parts of Great Britain, and, thanks to *The Studio*, in Europe. Their first exhibition at Liège in Belgium, 1895, encouraged the Secretary of L'Oeuvre Artistique to write to Newbery, noting, 'Our schools of art are far, very far indeed, from being so advanced as yours and what has above all astonished us in your work is the great liberty left to pupils to follow their own individuality which is so different from ... our schools.'

As a result of the interest generated in Liège, The Four were invited to exhibit at the London Arts and Crafts Society Exhibition in 1896 – a year considered by many to mark the height of the Glasgow Style. Their works on display consisted of metalwork panels, posters, a

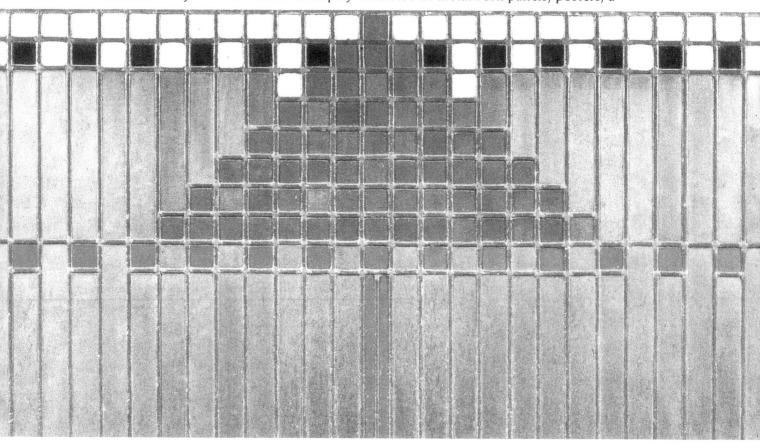

Mackintosh furniture design and a silver clock-case. Once again, their work was met with critical disdain, and identified wrongly with the Aesthetic movement. One critic described their work as 'the outcome of juvenile enthusiasm … absolute ugliness … a passion for originality at any price'. It was at this point that Gleeson White, Editor of *The Studio*, began his crusade in favour of The Glasgow Four and the Glasgow Style. He wrote the prophetic words, 'Probably nothing in the gallery has provoked more decided censure than these works, and that fact alone should cause a thoughtful observer of art to pause before he joins the opponents. If the said artists do not come very prominently forward as leaders of a school of design peculiarly their own, we shall be much mistaken. The probability would seem to be that those who laugh at them today will be eager to eulogize them a few years hence.' He travelled north to meet the four artists, and they formed a relationship which would draw The Four to the forefront of the artistic world. In the same way that Ruskin had championed the Pre-Raphaelites and Turner, so Gleeson took on The Four, featuring their work in two issues of *The Studio* in the summer of 1897. This thrust them into the limelight and resulted in enormous interest from the Continent, where form in architecture, art and the decorative arts was undergoing dramatic change.

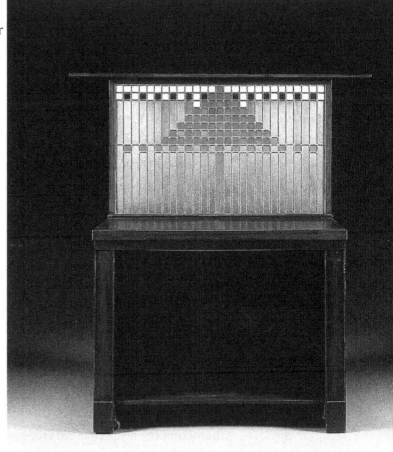

Mahogany Wash Stand.

Walter Blackie commissioned Mackintosh to design this piece to match an existing chest of drawers. It shows the characteristic coloured glass and pewter in the form of a stylized tree set into the unpainted wood.

The Studio also published the architecture of Voysey and the works of Walter Crane and Aubrey Beardsley alongside the work of The Four. When the critics challenged their artistic worth the magazine hotly defended its protégés. Many of the critics claimed that The Four, in particular the Macdonald sisters, could not draw, and that their sinuous images were the result of poor draughtsmanship rather than creative symbolism. Margaret later defended her work to Gleeson White, saying 'Certain conventional distortions, harpies, mermaids,

Floral and Chequered
Fabric Design.
*This black and white
chequered pattern contrasted
with the brightly coloured
floral design, was to become
a common feature of
Mackintosh's designs.*

caryatids and the rest are accepted, why should not a worker today make patterns out of people?'.

The critical debate surrounding The Four continued to grow, and there was constant speculation about their influences. Incessant identification of their work with Art Nouveau was a label which Mackintosh in particular despised, largely because he considered the group to be untouched by such influences. MacNair later said, 'The work of our little group was certainly not in the very least inspired by any Continental movements ... we knew little about these until we were well away on our own endeavours ...'. At one point it was decided that Egyptian art was their primary source, but this was soon discounted by Gleeson White, who insisted, and then proved, that they were much closer to contemporaries like Gustav Klimt, Edvard Munch and, in particular, Aubrey Beardsley, whose curvilinear patterns and spirituality were echoed in The Four's work. Celtic influence was evident in their designs as well, with convoluted patterns of plants and hair recurring in an ornate imitation of Celtic imagery. Beardsley's illustrations also called upon Japanese prints as a key influence, with a carefully orchestrated balance, and black and white contrasting to areas of plain and then complex and concentrated detail. These characteristics would eventually feature heavily in Mackintosh's own work.

But the curtains were closing on the successful partnership of The Four. In 1899, MacNair and Frances Macdonald married and moved to Liverpool where MacNair was appointed Instructor in Decorative Design at Liverpool University's School of Architecture. Mackintosh continued with his decorative commissions, and began the first of his great architectural projects: the new Glasgow School of Art. The Four was now two, and in 1900, Margaret Macdonald and Charles Rennie Mackintosh were married, beginning a new era of collaboration that would see their influence spread across the globe.

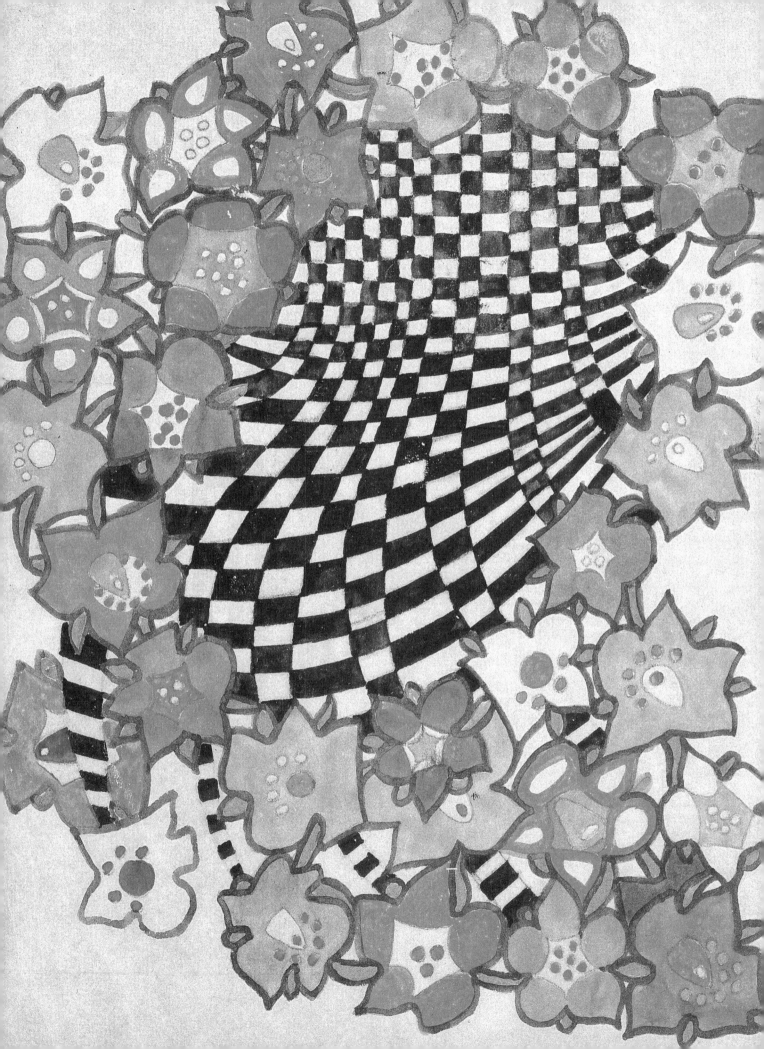

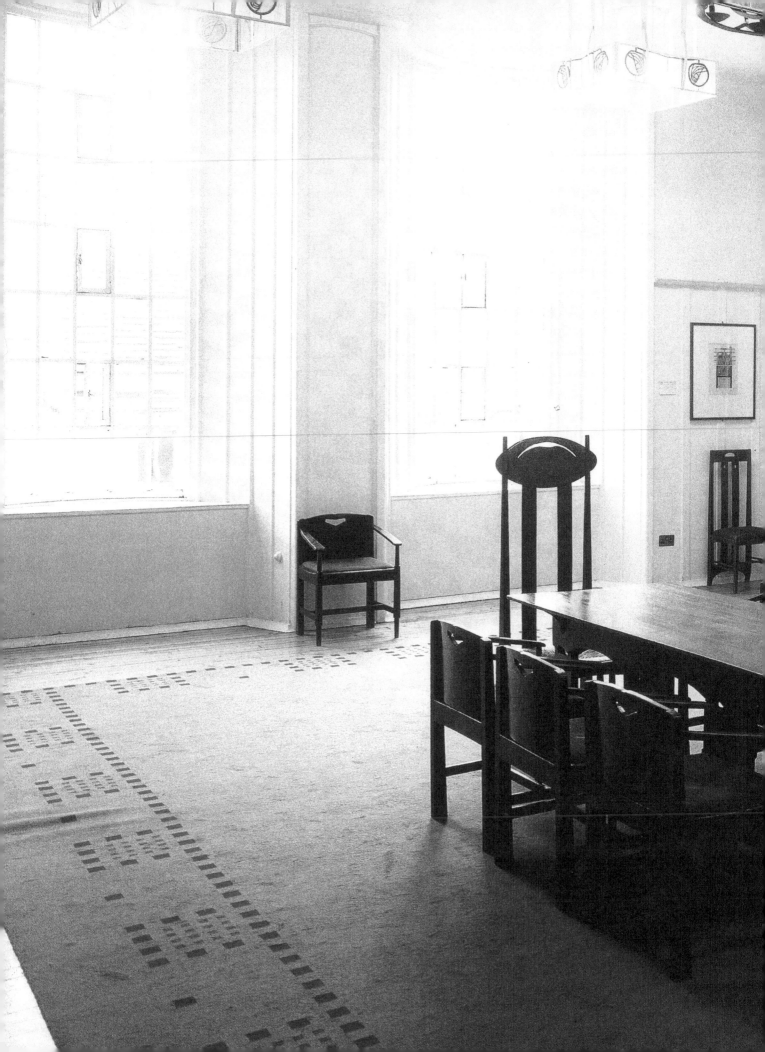

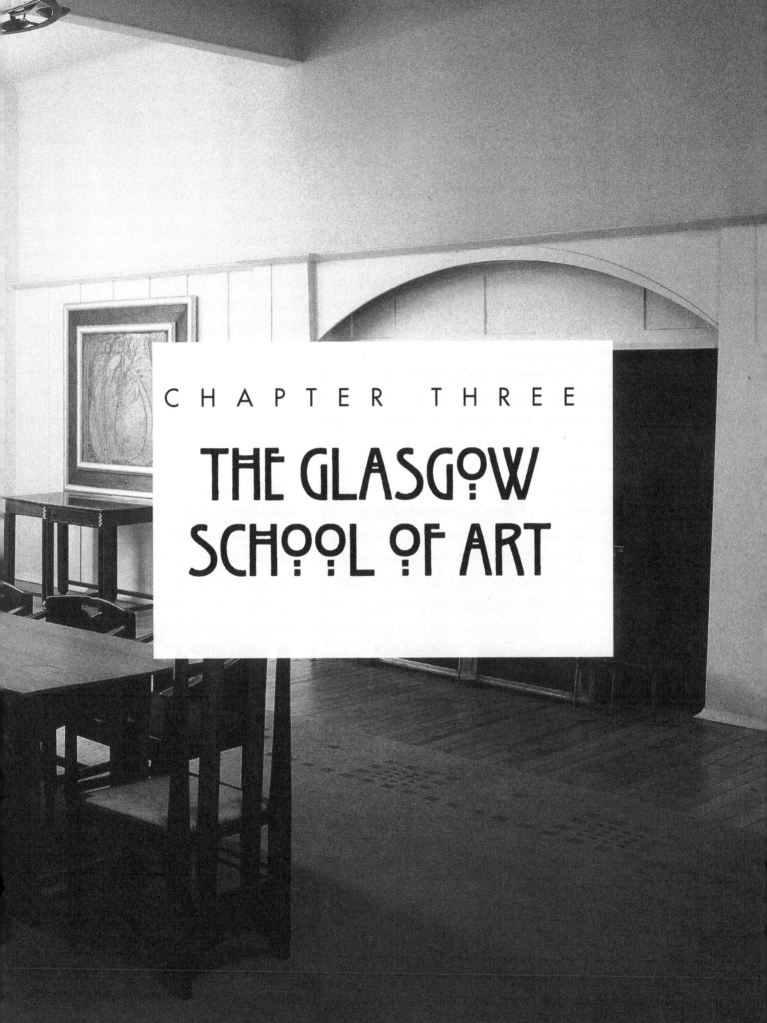

CHAPTER THREE

THE GLASGOW
SCHOOL OF ART

The appearance of the Glasgow Art School ... expresses the mind behind it. Here I feel that the tensions of the Scottish character find perfect synthesis: its wildness and austerity, its softness and ruggedness, come together in perfect proportion.

R. D. Laing

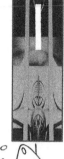

N THE FINAL YEARS of the nineteenth century, it was decided that the Corporation Galleries were no longer sufficient to house the Glasgow School of Art, and Francis Newbery, the School's director, called together a meeting of the governors to discuss fund-raising for a new building, one that would be 'sufficient for the present needs of the School'. In total, twelve architectural practices were invited to submit their plans for the new building, which was to be designed and built for £14,000.

Honeyman and Keppie was one of the practices chosen to compete for this coveted commission, and in 1897 their entry was chosen by the governors. The design was entirely that of twenty-nine-year-old Mackintosh, who planned a unique and charismatic structure, to be built on a difficult site of land called Garnethill, close to the heart of Glasgow. In a city that had come to expect Classical architecture and an ancient European approach, Mackintosh's designs were considered to be scandalous and insulting. He was slated for his austere approach, with its defiant lack of historical associations, and it was suggested that the building was over-large and too severe for a centre of art. Some critics called the proposed building over-modern, hinting once again at Art Nouveau which was largely disparaged in turn-of-the-century Glasgow, and others professed to see a Japanese influence, which was deemed inappropriate for a Scottish institution.

Mackintosh had created something new, and it was to become his masterpiece – being not only innovative and his largest project to date, but perhaps one of the most influential buildings ever constructed in Great Britain. He had supplied what the governors had requested: a plain, functional building created with the artist in mind. The building was a large, rectangular block, severe in appearance and asymmetrical, and Mackintosh called upon a number of Scottish themes from the baronial-medieval past to place it in context.

Mackintosh planned the building with a central E-shape, sitting on a rectangular foundation. The central core housed the circulation, administration, and services departments, with an entrance hall, head-master's room and studio, and museum taking up the heart of the

Glasgow School of Art, Front Entrance. *Mackintosh's plans for the new Glasgow School of Art were submitted through Honeyman and Keppie, the architectural practice for which he worked. Despite criticism about their 'modern' approach, they were accepted.*

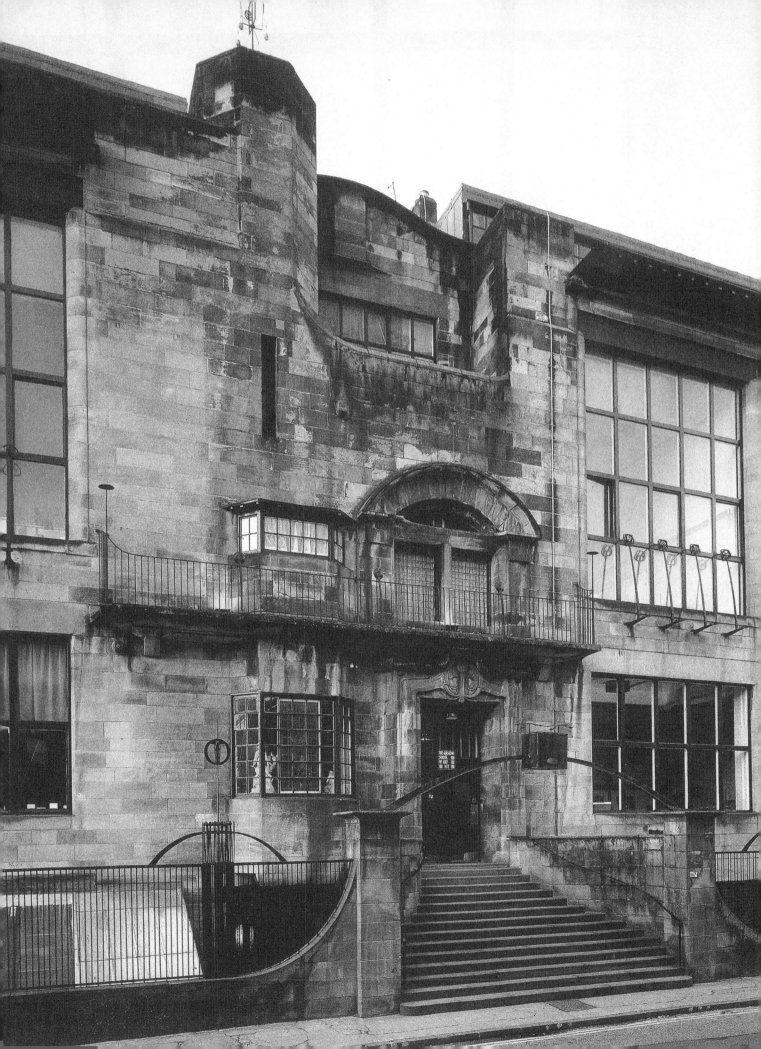

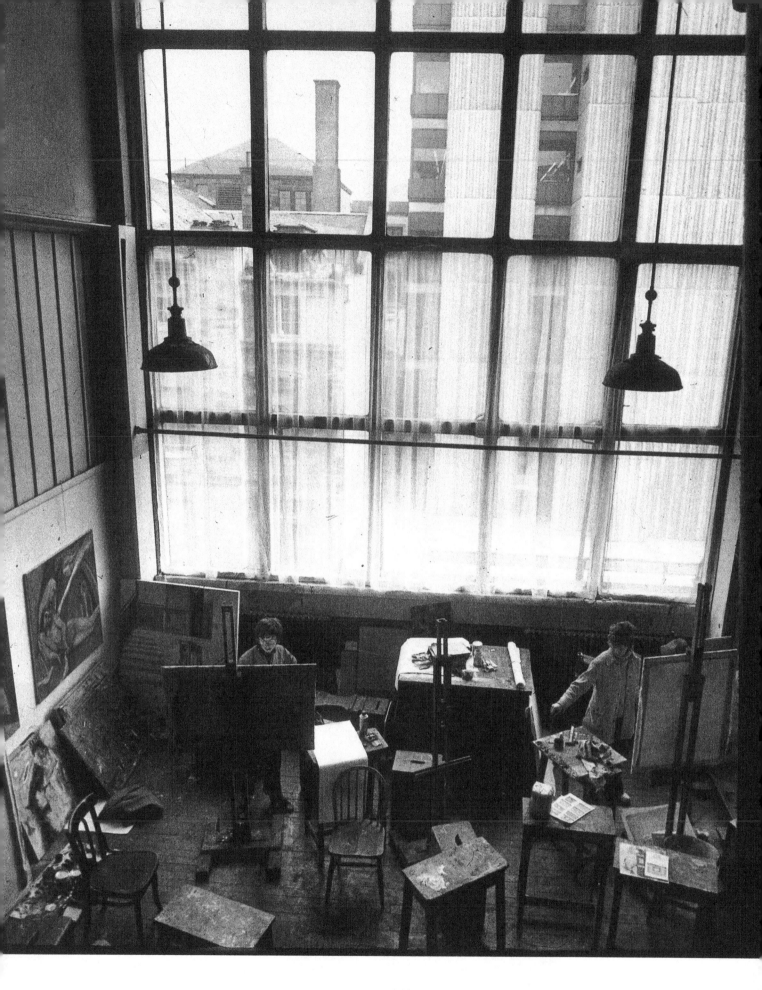

building. On either side, studios were arranged with large windows to take in the northern light. Modelling and architecture were given space in the basement; ornament, still-life and design were on the ground floor; and painting had the top, beautifully-lit floor of the school. Two outer wings, with five storeys each, were to house the boardroom and caretaker's house.

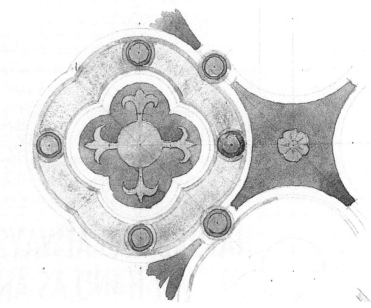

Ceiling Decoration in the Certosa di Pavia.
Sketches such as this detail of a ceiling decoration made during Mackintosh's travels through Italy were used in many of his later designs.

Although the proposed cost of the building work initially fell within the governors' brief, they could, in the end, only afford to build the central and eastern parts of the building in the 1890s, completing a newly designed west wing ten years later. The front of the building is divided exactly in the centre, by an entrance with a flight of stone stairs that meet curved walls at their base. Above that, a two-storey oriel sits slightly asymmetrically, intended to house a caretaker's cubby hole, and above that was the headmaster's lavatory. The headmaster's room lies over the entrance with a balcony crossing the oriel, and above that is his studio, set back and accessed by a stair tower. It was an inventive design, an example of Free Style architecture, with a variety of unusual features designed for effect, hiding the practical uses. The tower rises much higher than the staircase it encloses, and the studios have austere, but proportionally grand windows with differing widths and intervals between them. The railings on the entrance walls are also asymmetrical, but balanced around the centrepiece. The severity of the large windows is enhanced by delicate ironwork and braces, with floral knots of intertwined metal. Not merely decorative, these brackets were used to provide support for window cleaners' scaffolding and the bars of the windows.

The main entrance is framed by a deep, curved architrave, about which Alan Crawford, in *Charles Rennie Mackintosh*, notes, 'the mouldings rise into leaf-like forms or merge with the flowing hair and clothes of two women, who kneel in the central medallion with a stylized rose-bush between them. This is more than the graceful simplification of traditional mouldings which Free Style architects practised. There is ambiguity, as wall merges into moulding and moulding into imagery;

Studio in the Glasgow School of Art.
The artists' studios in the Glasgow School of Art were housed on the top floor, where the large windows provided perfect lighting for painting.

and there is a symbolic design typical of The Four, framing the entrance to their spiritual home.' The walls and steps were described as being 'welcoming and protecting arms' as one enters the building, and they were created with a castle moat in mind.

The face of the east wing was broken exactly in two by a downpipe, with the entrance and tower, and the majority of irregularly shaped windows on the left-hand side. Apart from two small, variously shaped windows which were added in 1915, the right-hand side of the façade was completely blank.

It is a building full of contrasts, which delighted the young designer with their subtlety and balance: high towers jut out from low façades, black is thrust against white, dressed stone against cement render, and the ultimate paradox – a melancholy, sedate building filled with brilliant light. The eastern elevation is Scotch Baronial in flavour, with windows of varying sizes, including arrow-slit windows. The entrance door is shielded by a small wall, which could be closed off to create a pen for the animals that Mackintosh proposed to use in 'the animal room', where students could study beasts firsthand.

NATURE WAS ALWAYS AT HAND AS AN INSPIRATIONAL SOURCE

When it was completed, years later, the western wing contrasted with the eastern wing through its sheer grandeur.

Anthony Jones wrote, 'All of this is in contrast with the western elevation, which rises in a similar way, but then soars like a fortress tower. Mackintosh here fuses his understanding of the totemic power of that Scottish form with his appreciation of the geometric and arithmetic logic of Japan, in the high narrow shoji-screen windows of the double-storey library within. At the top of the south-western elevation he cantilevered out a small greenhouse in which plants were grown, a giddy perch adjacent to the Plant Drawing Room, with its Japanese 'tori-like' complex of roof trusses. Nature was always at hand as an inspirational source.'

The doorway to the basement studios has an elaborate surround, with deep-set black doors. Jones writes, 'This hooded lintel is flanked at the top edges with crow steps (partly in recollection of castle architecture, but perhaps also a memory of the frontispiece of Lethaby's book, which showed a great stepped truncated pyramid) and in its geometrication it anticipates Art Deco.'

There was an eloquence of the design, and a continuity that

Certosa di Pavia, Studies of the Ceiling Decoration.

Although Mackintosh's time in Europe seemed purely to increase his appetite for traditional Scotch architecture, his travels and notebooks still fired his imagination.

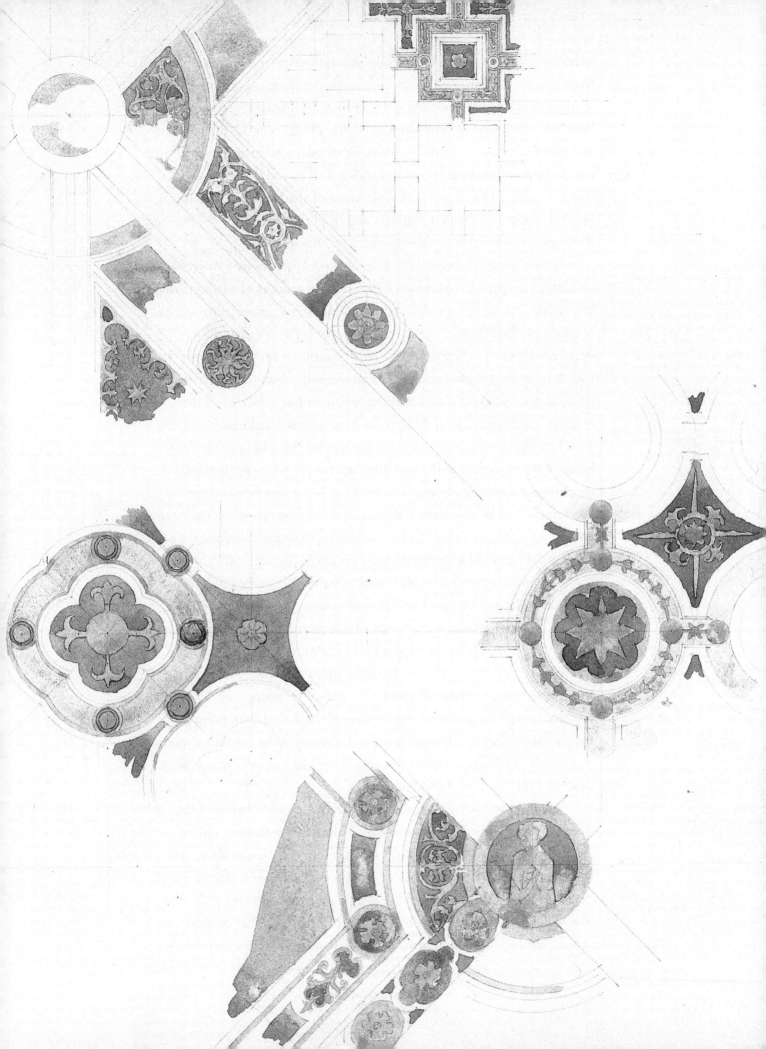

belied the fact that there were a jumble of differing influences at play, from the Scotch Baronial, to the medieval, the Japanese, and then the work of Mackintosh's own contemporaries, from whose designs he drew great inspiration. The work of Smith and Brewer, C. F. A. Voysey and Norman Shaw is recalled in various details, while the extraordinary metalwork, with animal forms and stylized trees and flowers is Mackintosh's own discreet personalization of the building. The metal brackets indicate a Celtic influence, and from the interior of the building they appear as beautiful and elaborate steel flowers.

James Steele, in *Synthesis in Form*, writes: 'If attribution of stylistic or cultural reference remains problematic, the sources of Mackintosh's historicism are no longer obscure, and while some connections appear tenuous and far-fetched, the game of tracing influences has yielded several solid clues ... the detective work continues on many fronts, to such a point that it has become an end in itself, obscuring the true significance of the synthesis that the architect has achieved in the process. Like Frank Lloyd Wright, to whom he is often compared, but who had the opportunity to evolve a personal language perhaps partly because his professional life was 30 years longer and was encouraged by patrons rather than being criticized for being too avant-garde, Mackintosh had an assimilative heuristic ability based on keen observation and memory. In each case, Gaudi's aphorism that orginality meant a return to origins was translated into a return to precedents.'

The interior of the building was as carefully contrived as the exterior, and it was reported in *The Studio* magazine as an 'exercise in the use of materials and technology of the period'. In contrast to the views of William Morris and John Ruskin, with whom Mackintosh normally shared sympathy, the building houses a wealth of machinery to produce a 'well-tempered' environment for the occupants. Cold air was drawn into the building, heated and filtered, and then pumped through shafts to provide movement and warmth in the grandiose rooms.

Anthony Jones, in his commentary on Mackintosh's major works, describes the interior of the building:

'The central staircase leads up from the entrance hall into the Museum, partly filled with plaster casts for drawing studies, with a pitched blazed roof flooding light into the interior. The scale recalls the Great Hall of medieval castles, or baronial mansions, but the subtle detailing implies that the staircase is a living forest of vertical shoots (the wider balusters have a pair of leaf-shaped perforations) culminating in four stylized 'trees' that grow upwards to appear to support the canopy of the roof ... on the Museum floor (the first floor) the axial corridors lead to the great painting studios on the north wall. The ceiling height is about twenty-seven feet ... with accordion doors that allow the conversion of several principal studios into one huge room .... The Director's office is designed as a multi-purpose, open-plan space essentially square in plan, with a deep offset bay window in the west ... this is one of the first of Charles' famous 'white rooms' that are imbued with a feeling of sensuous calm, accentuated here by the gently curving cornice at the top of the wall panelling, which dips and flows into the bay windows, and whose curves are replayed in the sweep of the panelling ... the room is notable for the way in which Mackintosh unites the design motifs of the grid pattern of nine squares, which became a leit motif for Mackintosh and which was also used widely by the Vienna designers under his influence. The grid is seen in the backs of the chairs designed for this room, and it is echoed in the legs of the circular table and again in the light fittings ...'.

The Boardroom was planned as a large rectangle, lit at both ends by tall windows, with a central fireplace taking up most of the southern wall.

Construction began on the western wing in 1907, finishing in 1909. Mackintosh's plans were always undertaken with growth in mind, and he was able to make the addition, effortlessly altering his original plan, to allow for the growing needs of the artistic community to expand into an organic and wholly united space.

The initial work on the School was overseen by Keppie, and not surprisingly he, and the firm, were given most of the credit for the work, particularly since Mackintosh still held a very junior position within the firm. He was beginning to make his own name, however, and while the work on the School was underway, he began a series of

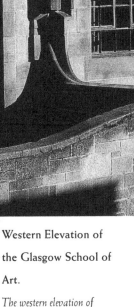

Western Elevation of the Glasgow School of Art.

The western elevation of the School was to be a magnificent construction, contrasting with the less grand eastern wing. Lack of funds meant, however, that it was not completed until ten years later.

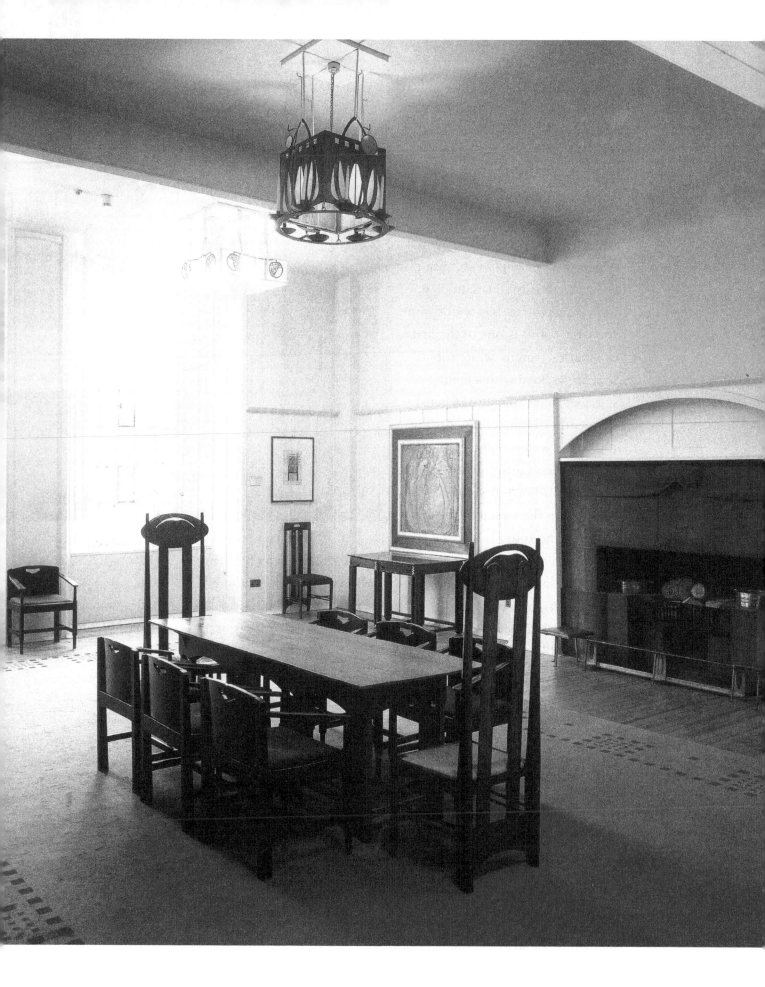

commissions that drew attention to his unique blend of perfect skill, inventiveness and vision. In 1898, Mackintosh was reported to have said, 'I hope when brighter days come, I shall be able to work for myself entirely and claim my work as mine.'

The core of the new wing of the School was its library, with a central space flanked by two rows of four wooden uprights, standing over two rolled steel joists. There are decorative features – short balustrades between a gallery and the uprights, which were enamelled in primary colours. The remainder of the library is a grove of trees, allowing Mackintosh to work with wood rather than metal – which was necessary for the structure of the room – and to toy once again with the Japanese influence.

The light fittings were made of metal, shaped and pierced and then soldered together, and they appear symmetrically and evenly throughout the room until they meet in a cascade of coloured glass in the chandelier in the Salon De Luxe. The windows are broken by a vertical band. Alan Crawford writes, 'He designed three light-giving oriels and then crossed them out. This was the culmination of all those frieze rails running across windows, and a stronger version of the pseudo-gallery in the Oak Room ... Mackintosh has dis-covered that plan and elevation do not have to go hand in hand, that there could be a gap between them, in which he loved to play. It was a strange notion, quite different from the real separation between the external wall and the internal structure which steel-frame construction made possible at this time.'

EVERYTHING IS JUST RIGHT AND IT SEEMS MORE RIGHT THE MORE ONE LOOKS AT IT

The decorative panels are repeated in the legs of the library tables and on the large desk in the centre of the room, each one expressing a different element of his central theme. R. D. Laing, educator and theorist, described it as 'a very congenial place to be in. Nothing cries out for attention, but everything is just right and it seems more right the more one looks at it. Correct without ever being cold. Those hanging lamp-shades are metal but they are not metallic. I wonder why the designers of our high-rise brutalism haven't taken a leaf from Mackintosh's book. But maybe they haven't loved, as he did, the flowers and plants that he spent so much time studying and drawing and painting as a boy. Somehow he manages to take metal and use it organically and poetically to express through it light and colour and delight.'

Boardroom in the Glasgow School of Art.

A large portion of one wall of the Boardroom is taken up with a fireplace. Mackintosh often used this as a symbolic element in his interiors, using plain surrounds with insets of coloured glass or tiles.

Library in the Glasgow School of Art.

The Library is one of the most impressive rooms in the School, and is characteristic of Mackintosh's holistic approach – the decorative motifs recur throughout the room, even on the legs of the tables.

The successful years that culminated in the construction of the west wing of the school fell onto fallow ground, and in the four years following the completion of his masterpiece, few commissions were offered. The fortunes of Mackintosh, and the firm of Honeyman and Keppie began to decline. Added to this were Keppie's and Mackintosh's irreconcilable differences, based mainly on the jilting of Jessie Keppie, which was considered heartless, as well as being scandalous in Victorian England. Mackintosh began to drink heavily, having invested so much in his work, his art, his reputation and in his relationship with Margaret. Although little is known about their actual relationship, for Mackintosh was not a man accustomed to keeping accurate and regular journals, their collaboration drew them to the forefront of the artistic community both in Scotland and abroad, and stories abound about the talented artist and architect, and his flame-haired older wife.

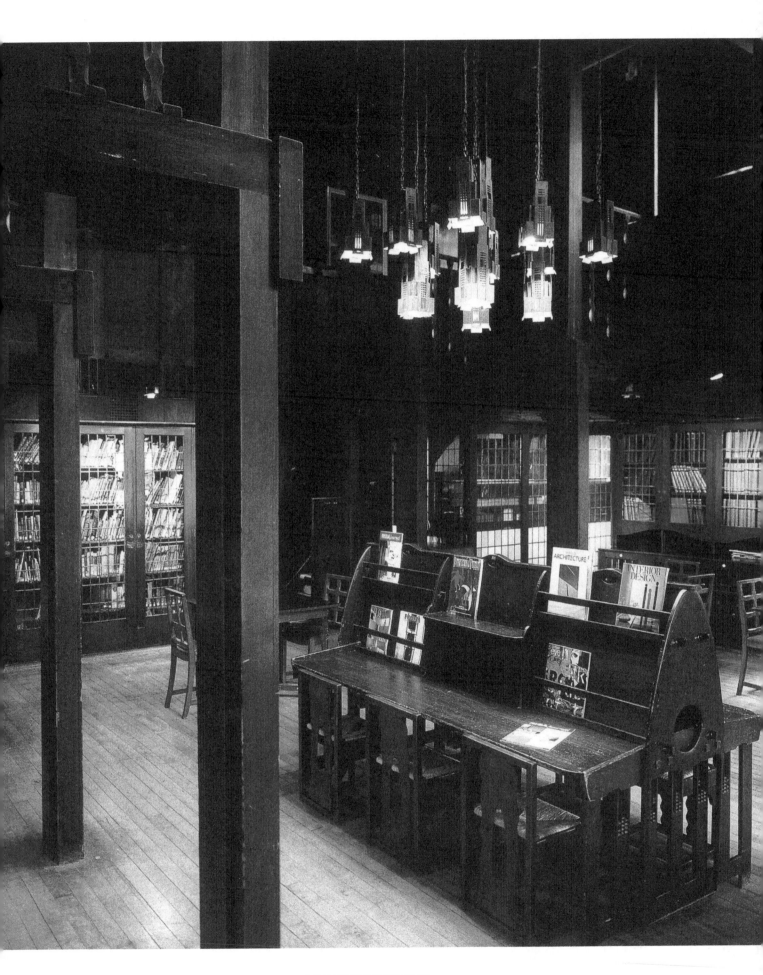

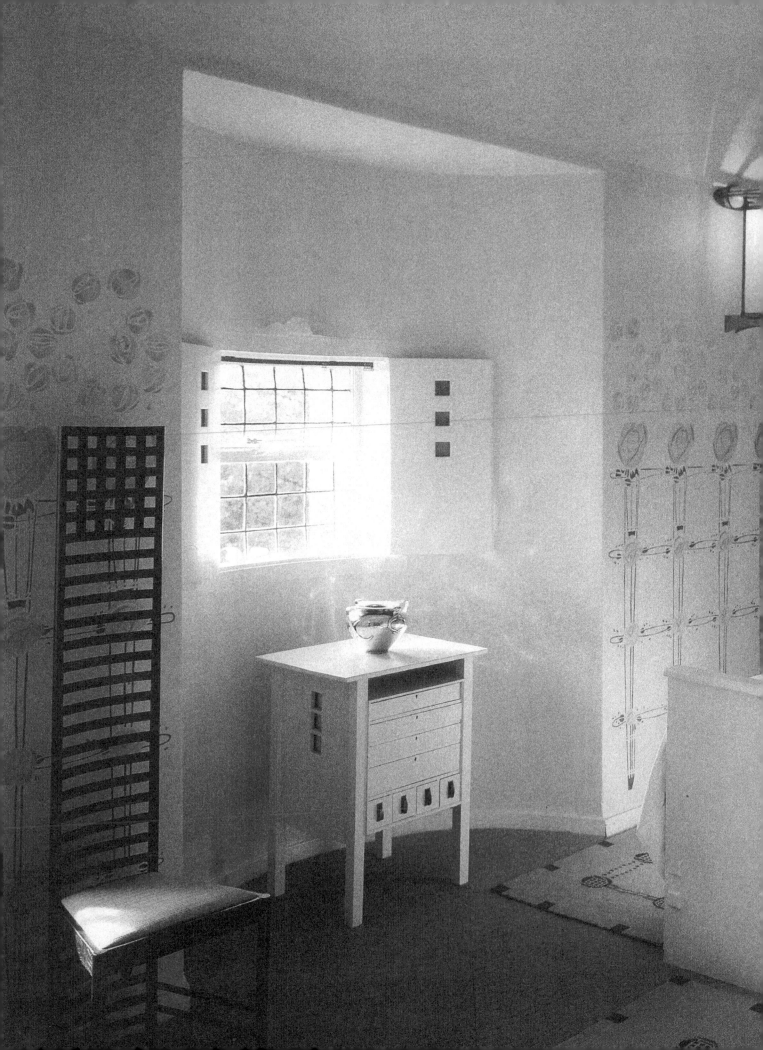

CHAPTER FOUR

THE PERFECT PARTNERSHIP

Margaret has genius, I have only talent.

Charles Rennie Mackintosh

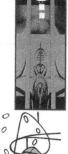

N 22 AUGUST, 1900, Charles Rennie Mackintosh married Margaret Macdonald: a stately middle-class woman with a calm air and a luxurious mass of auburn hair. Her composure was often mistaken for aloofness, but she was the perfect match for the feisty, industrious Mackintosh who had spent most of his life in an ever-growing family and longed for serenity and the kind of simplicity that Margaret could easily match. Margaret had grown up in a quiet household, the daughter of a Scottish father and an English mother. She had spent her childhood and early adulthood in the English Midlands, and upon moving to Glasgow had enrolled, with her sister Frances, in the School of Art, where their eccentric and highly skilled work made them an instant success.

The early years of Mackintosh's marriage were perhaps the most creative and inspiring of his working life. Their first home, at 120 Mains Street, offered Mackintosh his first opportunity to create the ideal living space, and Margaret was an impeccable foil for his artistic vision.

During the next few years, interiors and furniture design were to form the main part of Mackintosh's output and from here his work became inextricably linked to that of his new wife, whose influence is felt in everything he created. We will probably never know the full extent of their partnership, but their new home presents a picture of how the two creative talents worked as one.

At the beginning of 1900, they began to decorate and furnish their first-floor flat in an early Victorian building. They created a drawing room and a studio from the two largest rooms, which had high ceilings and tremendously large windows that allowed the light to pour into the open spaces. In the drawing room they divided the walls and ran a frieze rail around the room and across the windows. They boxed in an existing fireplace with planks and hung the windows with delicate muslin that enhanced the effect of the light coming through the glass. The atmosphere was simple – spartan and yet supremely elegant, with a judicious use of colour and line to create a somehow sensuous feel. The Mackintoshes chose a soft grey carpet, and enamelled white woodwork accented by purple squares in the frieze and purple glass in the gas light-fittings. The furniture represented a variety of Mackintosh's existing designs, but a new bookcase and

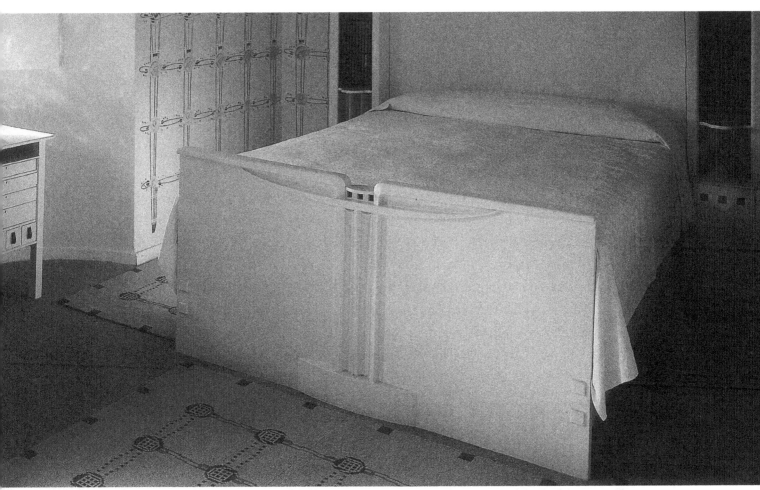

modelled desk, as well as a big chair with stylized trees were created
specially for the room. Japanese prints were propped against the walls,
and dried clematis curved up from a central vase.

In contrast to the light drawing room, the Mackintoshes created
a dark dining room, with brown paper below the frieze rail and dark
woodwork. Alan Crawford, in *Charles Rennie Mackintosh*, commented on
the interplay of dark and light that became the focus for much of the
Mackintoshes' work at the time: 'It was common in late 19th-century
middle class houses for the drawing room and bedrooms, which were
thought of as feminine, to be light in colour, while the dining room,
study, billiard room and smoking room, which were thought of as
masculine, would be sober, even dark. For some years from 1900, male
and female, light and dark, would become primary and fruitful
oppositions in the Mackintoshes' work.'

Their bedroom was smaller, and Mackintosh had produced two
cupboards with intricate moulding, and a cheval mirror lined by small
compartments. Once again, the feminine room was white, with an
extraordinary four-poster bed as a central feature. The inserts in the
foot of the bed sparkled with colour, and there were coloured panels in

**Master Bedroom
at Hill House.**
*Bedrooms were thought of as
feminine rooms, and were
designed to be light in
colour; rooms perceived as
masculine contained dark
wood and wallpaper. The
interplay of dark and light
can be seen in many of
Mackintosh's interiors
including Hill House
and the Tea Rooms.*

the frieze that echoed the bright dashes of colour that stood starkly against the white backdrop. The bed-clothes were also coloured, and they hung in the enclosed wooden bed which formed its own luxurious and private chamber.

There were powerful motifs dotted throughout the flat, and some experts have suggested that they present images of sexuality, fertility and the fecundity of nature. The lines are organic, dipping and swirling in glorious natural patterns, while motifs of delicate flowers and leaves, along with peacock tails, branches and roses creep across the exquisitely modelled furnishings and fittings. The juxtaposition of Mackintosh's now well-known use of line and formal approach and Margaret's more romantic, spiritual work created an atmosphere that was at once uncluttered, sparse and full of grace and erotic movement. This room has been put together and is on view in the Hunterian Art Gallery in Glasgow, and the peace and elegance that characterized their early days in the flat are still tangible today.

It must have seemed an odd flat, for it lacked any personal

THE EFFECT OF THE ENTIRE FLAT WAS ONE OF ART RATHER THAN LIVING

belongings or evidence of the home life of the Mackintoshes, and many people commented on its unrealistic and almost in-different character. The effect of the entire flat was one of art rather than living, and even the most functional pieces were created to present a unified whole. It was Mackintosh's ultimate holistic interior, produced for effect, one felt, rather than function. Muthesius called it a 'fairy-tale world' in which 'a book in an unsuitable binding would disturb the atmosphere simply by lying on the table', but Anthony Jones quotes the French writer, E. B. Kalas, who described it as a place of 'virginal beauty', inhabited by 'two visionary souls in ecstatic communion'.

Mackintosh was deeply attached to Margaret, and her romantic inclinations complemented his own more formal approach. She was devoted to symbolism, which he adopted in his work, and they shared a love of the writings of Rossetti, William Morris and Maurice Maeterlinck. Mackintosh integrated her paintings – which tended towards the mystical and nostalgic rather than the natural world as his did – and her metal panels into a number of the architectural works he created, and he was generous with his credit, calling her his muse and his ultimate inspiration.

Still Life of Anemones.
Many critics claimed that Margaret had too much influence over Charles' work and that their styles became indistinguishable. Pictures such as this still life, very different from the Macdonalds' 'Spook School' images, prove that Charles' style was very much his own.

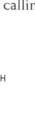

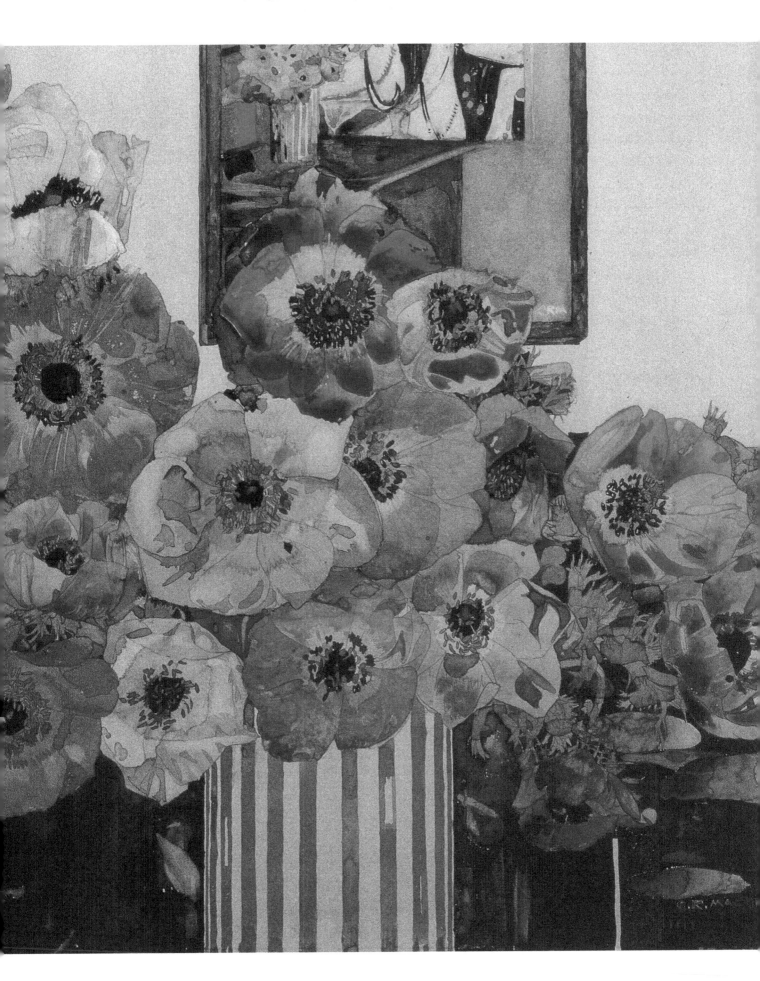

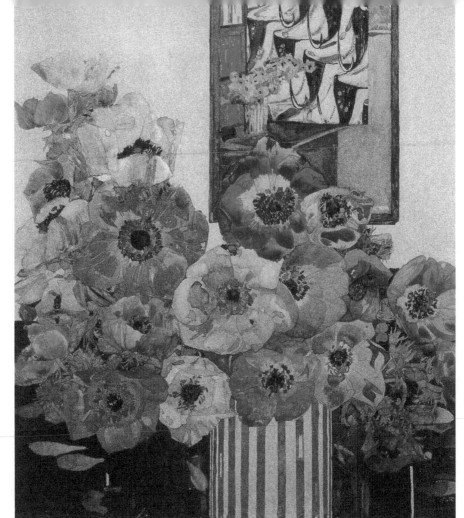

Some critics blamed Margaret for influencing him towards her own approach, but this opinion was not generally shared. Certainly, his output of work declined after several years of marriage, but his most creative period was that of their early marriage, and she was not involved in everything he did – merely clarifying his ideas and sharing his spirit. Margaret's work concentrated on appearance, while Mackintosh was forced to consider structure and functionability in his designs. For that reason, their beliefs had to be diverse, even if they were complementary.

Margaret's work was appreciated in its own light, and she was an overwhelming influence on the Glasgow Style, which she continued to practice in even her latest work. Many believe that her best works were those she produced in association with Mackintosh until about 1909, particularly her metal and embroidery, and the stunning gesso work which recalled her preoccupation with the medieval world. Mary Sturrock described the partnership between Mackintosh and Margaret thus: 'Mackintosh was an architect first and foremost, his line was our architects' line. When they say that Margaret was such an influence on him. well, it's just not true. She did all those wiffly watercolours; how could they have influenced somebody who thought structurally and in thin hard lines? She liked Toorop, Beardsley, Rossetti, and she painted fairy tales, even when she was older. She should have known better, perhaps. But she was a terrific person, they both were. Very clean, very hardworking, very fastidious. She made her work in the studio in the house and was very neat, never spilled a drop, and wore white cotton gloves .... She was Mackintosh's complete and splendid support, he couldn't have had a better wife, she gave him a beautiful, clean and peaceful house and he was completely sympathetic with her work, so he really did like to have those decorated paintings in the houses he designed.'

By all accounts, the very private Mackintoshes had a warm and loving relationship, sharing an affection for children, although they did not have any of their own. Their art became their offspring, and even when times became difficult, which they eventually did, and when the critics were less than approving, they took great solace in one another and the little world they had created within their own four walls. It was a perfect partnership, from an artistic, spiritual and affectionate point of view, and both parties thrived in its uncluttered midst.

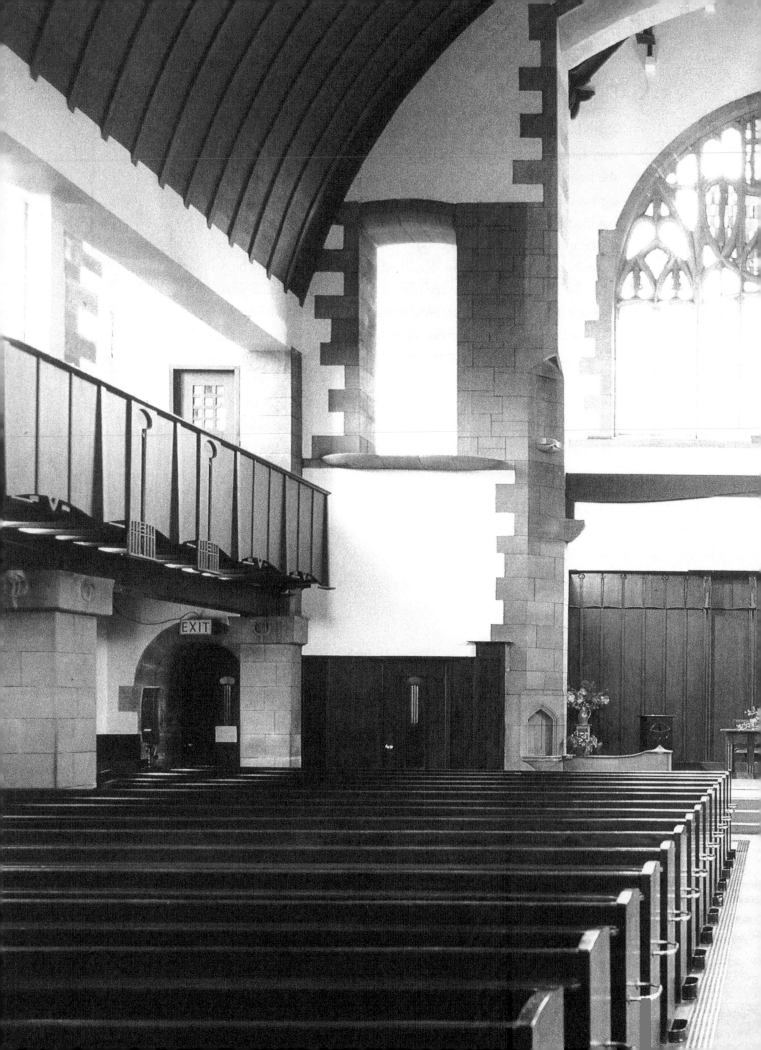

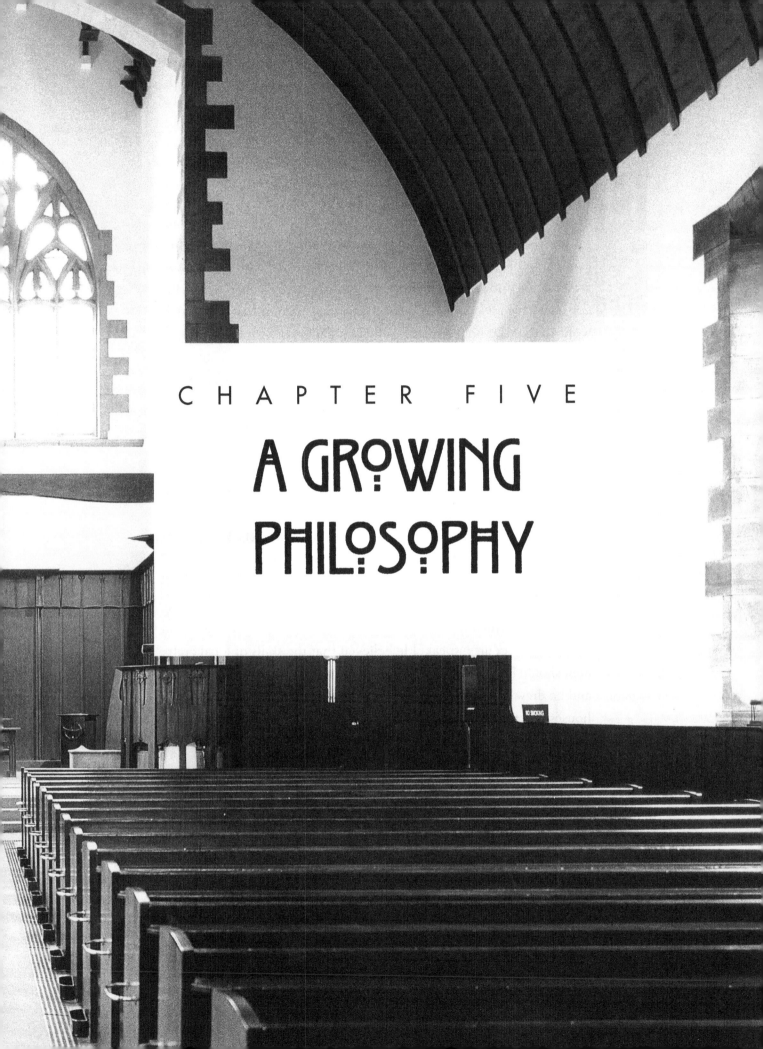

CHAPTER FIVE

A GROWING
PHILOSOPHY

*All the great and living architecture has been the direct expression of the
needs and beliefs of Man at the time of its creation. How absurd it is to
see modern churches, theatres, banks, all made in imitation of Greek
temples. There are many such buildings in Glasgow but to me they are
as cold and lifeless as the cheek of a dead Chinaman.*

Charles Rennie Mackintosh

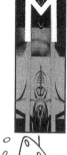

MACKINTOSH'S lecture on the Scotch Baronial style in 1891 remains
his most famous. It was both explorative and borrowed from the theories
of some of his favourite idealists. He propounded that nature, history,
architecture and cultural identity were a single factor that should be
considered in all artistic creation. Of course, most of Mackintosh's own
work to date did not express this theory, and most of his prize-
winning designs were based on Classical inspirations. His youth and
his enthusiasm, however, were enormously inspiring and his lecture
did serve the purpose of reminding his audiences – largely composed
of architects and artists – that it was possible to revive something
other than Classicism, and that their own heritage was more suited to
their environment and their needs.

Upon his return from his Italian tour, Mackintosh gave a further
lecture, discussing his travels and exhibiting his drawings, which
received some respectable attention from the critics. Mackintosh's trip
had inspired in him a lust for travel, and although the journeys he
undertook were now more local, exploring Scotland and England over
the coming years, he realized that the details of even the most basic
structures provided him with a wealth of material on which he could
draw, and, of course, speak. He believed that the skills of local craftsmen should be celebrated, in keeping with William Morris' thinking,
and he drew the most mundane of features from buildings such as out-
houses, churches, barns, taverns and manor houses. His travels in
England brought him into further contact with the main proponents of
the Arts and Crafts Movement, and with the teachings of W. R.
Lethaby, a prodigious talent in design.

In 1893, Mackintosh delivered a lecture based primarily on
Lethaby's book, *Architecture, Mysticism and Myth*, published in 1892,
which attributed a kind of philosophy to architectural expression.
Mackintosh found Lethaby's approach to modernism both inspiring
and essential to his beliefs, and his lecture was not only a tribute but
also a blatant appropriation of the other's ideals. He said: 'all the great
and living architecture has been the direct expression of the needs and

**Design for a
Dining Room.**
*Although Mackintosh was
striving to create a new
aesthetic mode,
many of his prize-winning
designs were still based on
Classical influences. This
design was entered in a competition for a modern art
lover's house, for which he
won a 'special Purchase
Prize' (see page 67).*

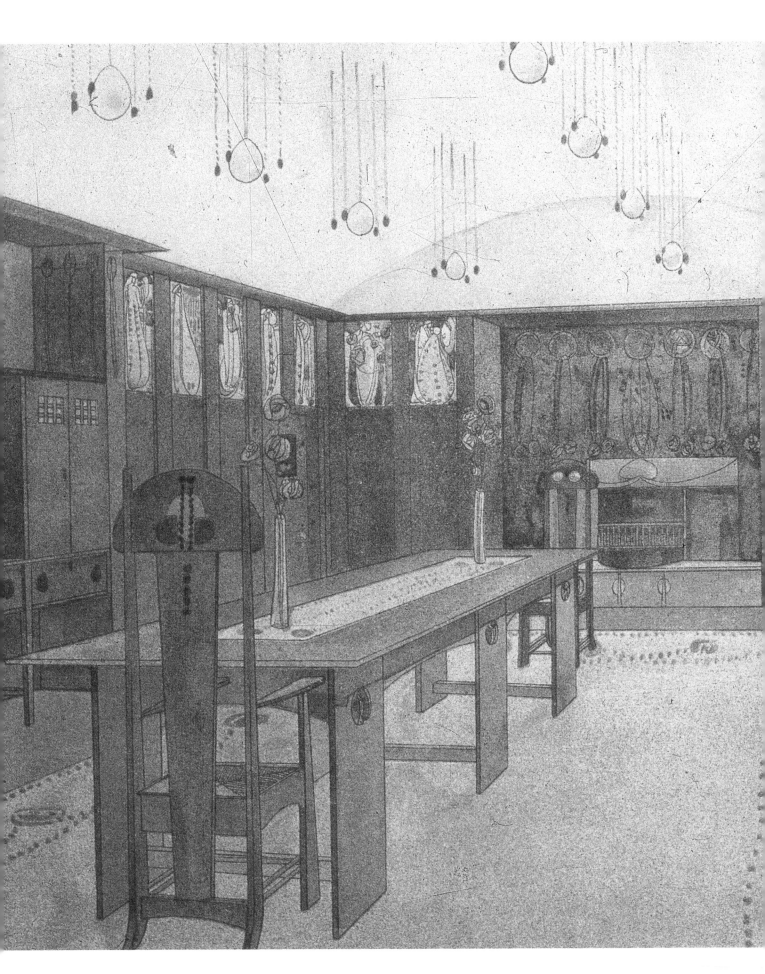

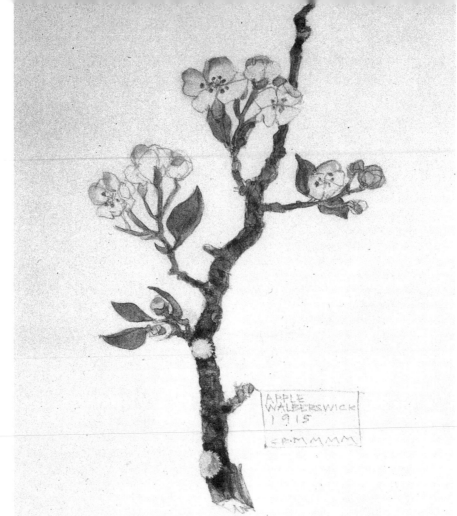

beliefs of Man at the time of its creation …. We must clothe modern ideas with modern dress – adorn our designs with living fancy. We shall have designs by living men for living men – something that expresses fresh realization of sacred fact – of personal broodings of skill – of joy in nature in grace of form and gladness of colour ... old architecture lived because it had a purpose: modern architecture, to be real, must not be a mere envelope without contents.'

Although Mackintosh liberally applied the Arts and Crafts ideology to his own theories, he did not, in practice, take them on board. He did not believe in decoration for its own sake, relying instead on the symbolic value of everything he used. Nor did he promote craftsmanship for its own sake, for he believed that the virtue of a piece of art was its visual statement. He was concerned with the overall appearance and the aesthetic rather than the means by which it was produced. Indeed, even William Morris was scathing about Mackintosh's talents, noting that his use of white painted furniture was surely evidence that Mackintosh was not a true craftsmen – a fact which is belied by his considerable attention to detail, reflected in all elements of design and his use of local artisans. But Mackintosh stressed that all details, including those of the furniture, are integral to a building's over-all appearance.

The wealth of material he digested presented Mackintosh with a cornucopia of ideas and theories, many of which he used in whole or in part, and others which he dismissed outright. There is no doubt that he himself was an important influence on the Art Nouveau style, but he was not, as we now know, in favour of their use of ornament. He was reliant on Pictish and Celtic imagery for much of his symbolism, identifying with the pagan attitudes of the Celts who worshipped nature, and evolved a cult around the spirituality of trees. Trees were an important symbol for Mackintosh, and he used them throughout his career, particularly in the Glasgow School of Art, the Willow Tea Rooms, and in the carved decoration of the pulpit at Queen's Cross Church. His watercolours – *Tree of Personal Effort* and *Tree of Influence* – echo the Celtic belief in the Tree of Knowledge, and he would come to share this fascination for the pantheistic and mystical mythology with his wife Margaret.

The powerful Japanese influence on Glasgow as a whole was undoubtedly important in the realization of Mackintosh's convictions. The Glasgow Boys – a group of famous Glasgow artists, including James Gurthrie, E. A. Hornel, John Lavery and E. A. Walton – had drawn inspiration from Japanese art and although Mackintosh rebuked their art, he could not help but feel the impact of Japanese culture. It was something which had become an obsession in nineteenth-century Glasgow. The Glasgow designer Christopher Dresser, gave several lectures on the art of Japan, which would have filtered through to Mackintosh even though he was a youth at the time, and he did identify with the art and design of Japan, with its supremely uncluttered elegance. He used screens and painted wood to achieve a feeling of space, and to divide his rooms, and he used Japanese heraldic emblems in the iron screen of the Glasgow School of Art's northern face. The Japanese concept of yin and yang, that is the balancing of opposites, was evident in his contrasts – black with white, dark with light, feminine with masculine.

Mackintosh's final lecture, in 1895, was more focused, in line with his increased experience, but he spoke once again on 'architecture' in general. At the time, the Glasgow Style had attracted a large number

HE WAS RELIANT ON PICTISH AND CELTIC IMAGERY FOR MUCH OF HIS SYMBOLISM

The tree was an important
symbol for Mackintosh and
he used it in many of his
interiors, including the
Queen's Cross Church, where
it was employed in the carved
decoration of the pulpit.

of disciples, and Mackintosh himself was working a great deal on decorative commissions, alongside his articles at Honeyman and Keppie. His concept of holistic design had matured, and he had the backing of *The Studio* magazine and its editor. He was a self-assured artist, who had carved his place in the art, design and architectural worlds, and his lectures had given him a new confidence, which was important for a working-class man in a middle-class environment. The decorative arts had begun to play a more crucial role in his work, and he became known more as a decorative designer than as an architect. This design work served to heighten his profile – particularly in pastures new on the Continent – and to feed his growing interest in symbolism, and the possibilities that lay between the worlds of art and architecture. It was this new ground that would make his name.

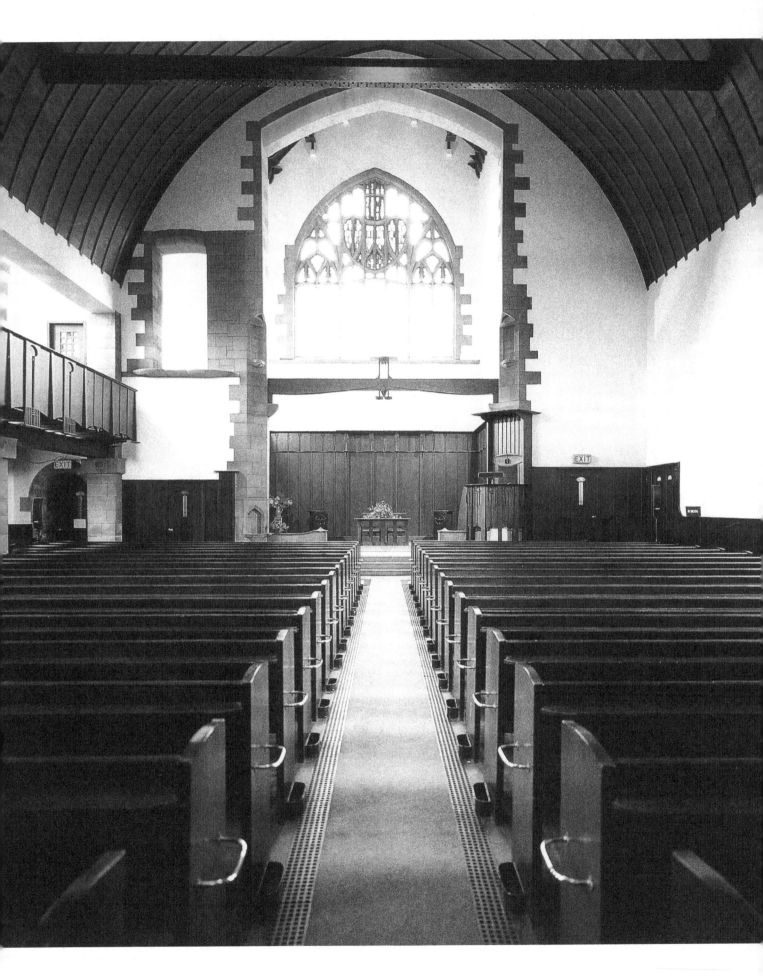

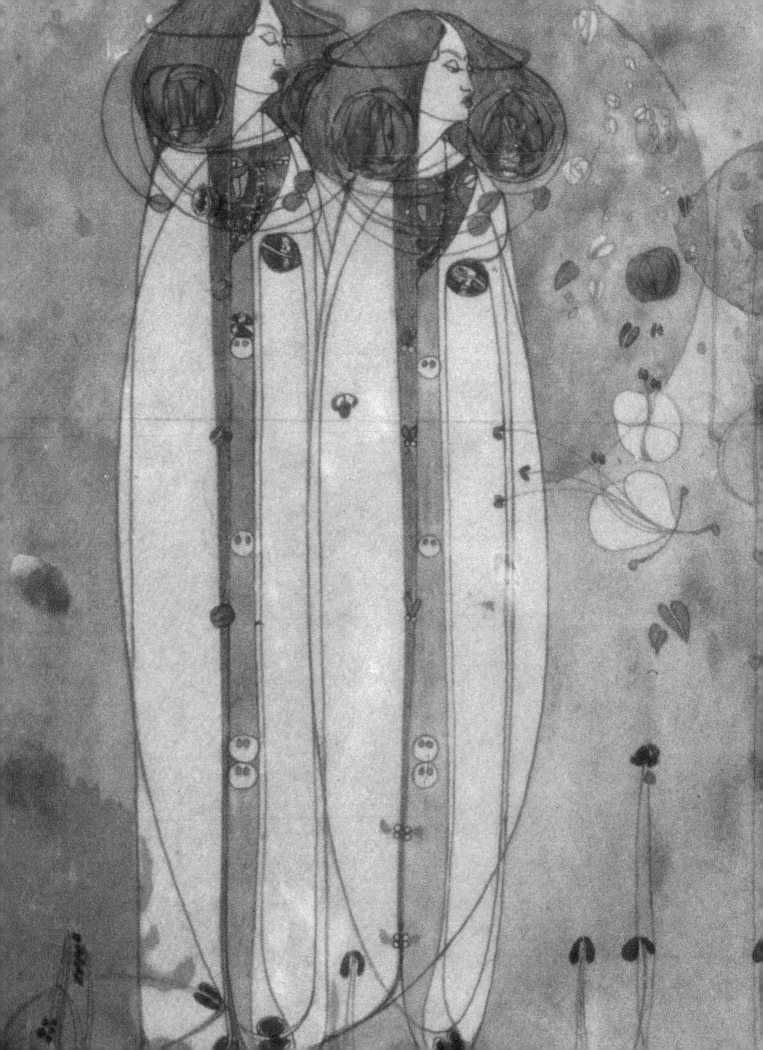

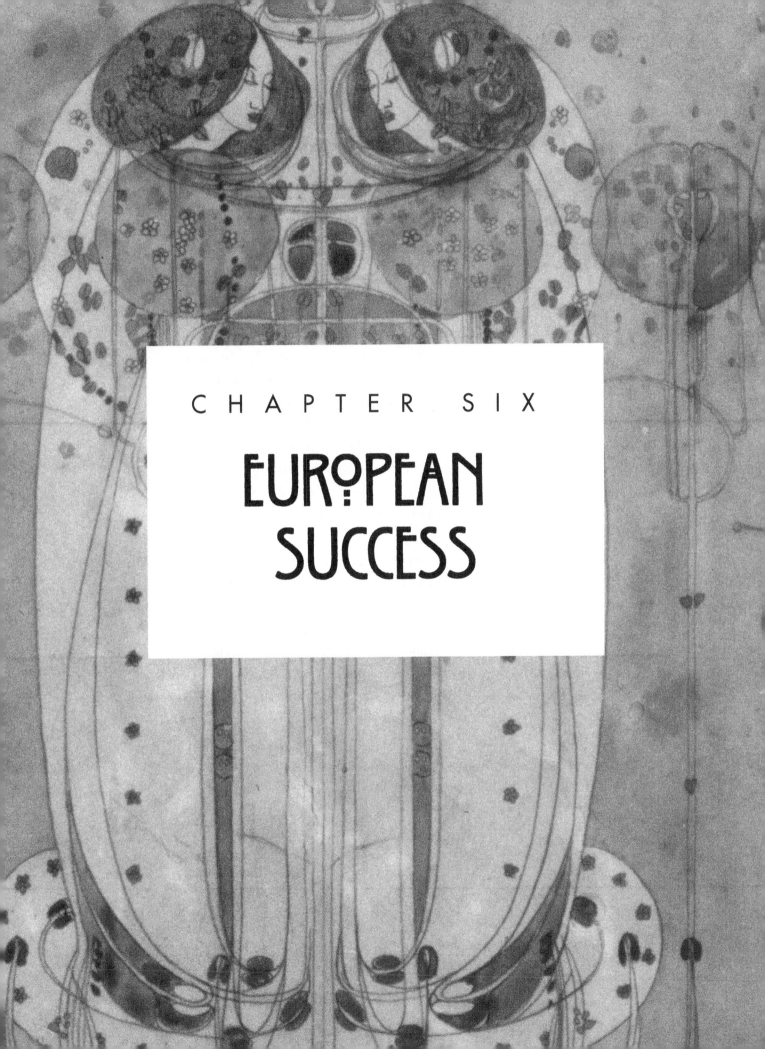

CHAPTER SIX

EUROPEAN SUCCESS

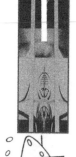

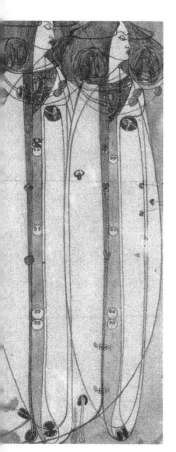

N THE AUTUMN of 1900, The Glasgow Four were invited to take
part in the eighth Secessionist Exhibition in Vienna; the Secessionists
announced that their aim was to 'impart appropriate form to modern
perception'. The work of The Four was already well-known on the
Continent, thanks to the efforts of Gleeson White, but White had
died in 1898, and his considerable support and patronage were not
replaced by anyone who identified quite so strongly with their vision.

Despite the previously icy reviews of their work, The Four
agreed to take part and produced, in collaboration, The Scottish
Room, which confirmed the shared ideology of The Four with the
Secessionists. The Vienna Secessionists had come together, along with
a similar movement in Germany, during the last decade of the nineteenth
century. Many of the more advanced German artists had found it
impossible to exhibit their works through the traditionally minded
organizations, so in 1892, they 'seceded' to found their own Munich-
based association and began to exhibit as a group. The leading members
in Munich were Franz von Stück and Wilhelm Trübner; their counterpart
Secessionists in Vienna were headed by Gustav Klimt, whose talents
encompassed applied arts and architecture as well as painting. The
Secessionists were believed to be the forerunners and the main proponents
of the Art Nouveau movement, which Mackintosh openly despised,
but their approach to art, and to architecture and furnishings as a
modern, united whole, were close enough to allow a good relationship
to form between the Scottish contingent and the Viennese.

Hermann Muthesius, a German architect and cultural attaché in
London, had an affinity with the young Scottish designers, and he
became Mackintosh's greatest patron and supporter on the Continent,
as well as an authority on Mackintosh's life and work, particularly after
his death. After the Exhibition, he wrote, 'they had a seminal influence
on the emerging new vocabulary of forms, especially and continuously
in Vienna, where an unbreakable bond was forged between them and
the leaders of the Vienna movement.'

Mackintosh's work had a dramatic influence on the Viennese
style, and he was hailed by the architect Joseph Hoffmann, who was
the driving force behind the initial Exhibition. The Mackintoshes

were welcomed in Vienna, a city of progressive artists and architects, and the *Neues Wiener Tagblatt* called their exhibit 'among the most striking achievements which modern art has created'. Mackintosh later said that this trip to Vienna was the high point of his life.

The Scottish Room was painted white, with tapered posts and a frieze rail dividing the walls. Framed watercolours and illustrations were hung on the walls, and the panels from the Ingram Street Tea Rooms faced one another above the rail. The furniture was a combination of pieces from the Mackintosh's home in Main Street, and others were created specially for the exhibition, but overall the effect was one of deliberate use of lines with restrained ornamentation, which adhered faithfully to the spirit of the competition.

The reviews themselves were mixed, despite Muthesius' approval, and some of the most progressive critics called the entry 'a hellish room ... no better than a torture chamber', with 'furniture as fetishes'. But even the most grudging of critics agreed that Mackintosh in particular was talented, and his work greatly influenced that of the Viennese – in particular his geometric motifs, lattice-work panelling and painted white surfaces. Klimt himself was significantly influenced, and the designs lor his wonderful *Beethoven Frieze* of 1902 were stylistically inspired by Margaret Macdonald Mackintosh's gesso panels. Equally the artistic delights of Vienna had an enormous impact on Mackintosh's work.

While they were in Vienna, the Mackintoshes were recommended to take part in a competition for the design of a large country house for an art-lover. The event was organized by the Darmstadt publisher, Alexander Koch, and the deadline was 25 March 1901. The house was to be modern, incorporating the art within the interior, rather than in a separate gallery.

The Mackintoshes' submission was disqualified on technical grounds because the required number of interior perspectives had not been included, but the judges were generally disappointed by the quality of the entries, which fell short of the avant-garde approach they had hoped for. For this reason, no first prize was given, and despite their disqualification, the Mackintoshes were awarded a 'special Purchase Prize' of 600 marks, a tribute to the radical break with tradition that the Art Lover's House presented. There was a horizontal linear emphasis in the design, which was carried into the rooms inside, joined by extensive corridors. The

The Wassail.

The Wassail is rendered in pencil, watercolour and bodycolour on oiled tracing paper. It was displayed as part of The Scottish Room at the eighth Viennese Secessionist Exhibition, where The Glasgow Four made a great impression in 1900.

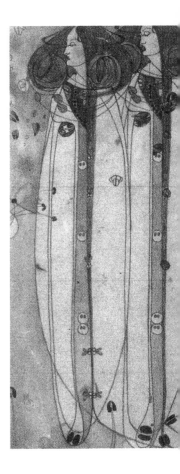

White Cabinet with Painted Decoration.

The geometric motifs and white painted surfaces that were a familiar element of Mackintosh's designs had a great effect on the Viennese at the Exhibition. His time in Vienna also had an enormous impact on Mackintosh's work.

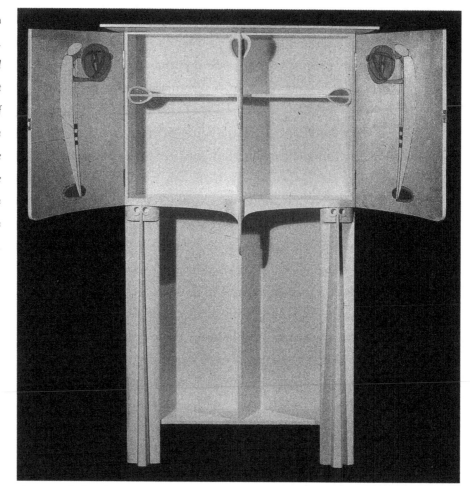

design of the Art Lover's House was said to indulge Mackintosh's fantasy of recreating an ocean liner on land, a legacy of the powerful ship-building industry in Glasgow at the time. Once again, however, the reviews were not unanimous in support of Mackintosh's approach, and the impressive linearity was considered to be too abstract, and lacking in humanity and the individuality that would characterize his next great residential projects, Windyhill and Hill House, in Glasgow. It was, however, an important competition, and it established firmly his international reputation as one of the most progressive architects of the day.

As a result of his heightened credibility, Mackintosh received a number of important international commissions. In 1898 he was hired to produce a dining room for H. Brückmann in Munich, who had been converted to the Mackintosh approach by the coverage in *The Studio*. In 1900, Fritz Warndorfer, the principal financial patron of the Secessionists, commissioned him to design a music salon, on the basis of the work he had exhibited in Vienna. The room was completed in 1902, decorated in characteristic white, with small lilacs and roses. The salon contained an immense grand piano, and beautiful panels painted by Margaret, based on Maeterlinck's *The Seven Princesses*. There were high-backed chairs echoing a design that Mackintosh had produced for the Kingsborough Gardens home in Glasgow, and the light fixtures were dramatic clusters of hanging lamps, almost like inverted flowers. *The Studio* drew attention to the room in 1912, writing, 'The composition forms an organic whole, each part fitting into the rest with the same concord as do the passages of a grand symphony; each thought resolves itself as do the chords in music till the orchestration is perfect, the effect of complete repose filling the soul'.

Warndorfer later purchased a few pieces of Mackintosh furniture, including a writing cabinet from the Rose Boudoir at the International Exhibition of Modern Decorative Art, Turin, in 1902.

The Viennese regarded Britain as a veritable garden of experimental and creative artistry: they enjoyed their idealist approach to the applied arts, architecture and design, and they applauded Mackintosh's holistic approach, which echoed their own beliefs. Warndorfer himself had visited Britain in the early 1890s, and had become widely indoctrinated with the views of Morris, Ruskin and the Arts and Crafts Movement. The Viennese believed in much the same principals, with Josef Hoffmann writing in *Der Architekt* in 1897: 'It is to be hoped that some time with us too, the hour will strike when one orders the wallpaper, the ceiling painting, the furniture and utensils not from the dealer but from the artist. England is far ahead of us in this ... we should recognize their interest in decorative arts and thus in art in general and we should strive to awaken it equally in us.'

Over the years between 1900 and 1906 Mackintosh represented the 'English movement' in Moscow, Budapest, Berlin, Turin, Munich and Dresden, and the Hungarians commented in *Magyar Iparmuvgszet* in 1902, 'In British decorative art, the centre of gravity has moved from London to Glasgow'. The 1901 edition of *Ver Sacrum*

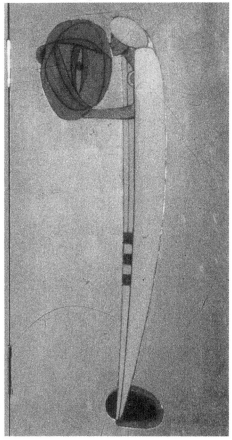

Detail from White Cabinet with Painted Decoration.
This stylized rose motif was a recurring theme throughout Mackintosh's interiors. When designing a room, he would plan details such as this to create a holistic feeling, and would repeat the colours and patterns in all elements of the furnishings.

(*Sacred Spring*, the Secessionist periodical) was devoted largely to the work of the Mackintoshes.

In 1903, Waerndorfer and his family backed a project initiated by Josef Hoffman for a workshop company of artisans who would create everything from houses and furniture, to textiles and bookbinding. The basis for their company was the views of William Morris, who had written in 1886, 'I must ask you to extend the word Art beyond those matters which are consciously works of art, to take in not only painting and sculpture and architecture but the shapes and colours of all household goods ... and to extend it to the aspect of all the externals of life.' Various proponents of the Arts and Crafts Movement were examined, but it was Mackintosh with whom the Viennese chose to discuss their project, and Hoffmann visited him in Glasgow in 1902. Mackintosh agreed with the principals of the company, called 'The Werkstatte', which was based on the ideologies of Ruskin and Morris, and proposed to regain the culture of their forefathers, a consideration that was very close to Mackintosh's own heart. He wrote to Hoffman: 'I have the greatest possible sympathy with your idea and consider it absolutely brilliant. If one wants to achieve artistic success with your programme ...

IN BRITISH DECORATIVE ART, THE CENTRE OF GRAVITY HAS MOVED FROM LONDON TO GLASGOW

every object which you pass from your hand must carry an outspoken mark of individuality, beauty and the most exact execution. From the outset, your aim must be that every object which you produce is made for a certain purpose and place .... The plan which you ... have designed is great and splendidly thought out ... begin today! If I were in Vienna, I would assist you with a great strong shovel!' Mackintosh's work was shown again in 1903, although he did not attend the exhibition. His dear friend Josef Maria Olbrech – an Austrian architect who was also one of the founders of the Secession, for which he designed the first exhibition building in the Art Nouveau style – did exhibit, however, and took great pleasure in defending Mackintosh's style in Russia. He wrote to his wife, 'Today a journalist came to interview me but he was so stupid I sent him away. This foolish Russian critic allowed himself – in my presence! – to make fun of the work of Mackintosh.'

Mackintosh's influence continued to grow in Europe, although he did not leave Scotland again, and the personal friendships he had

The Art Lover's House.

The designs for the Art Lover's House were submitted in a competition while the Mackintoshes were in Vienna. Mackintosh is said to have designed the house as an ocean liner on land.

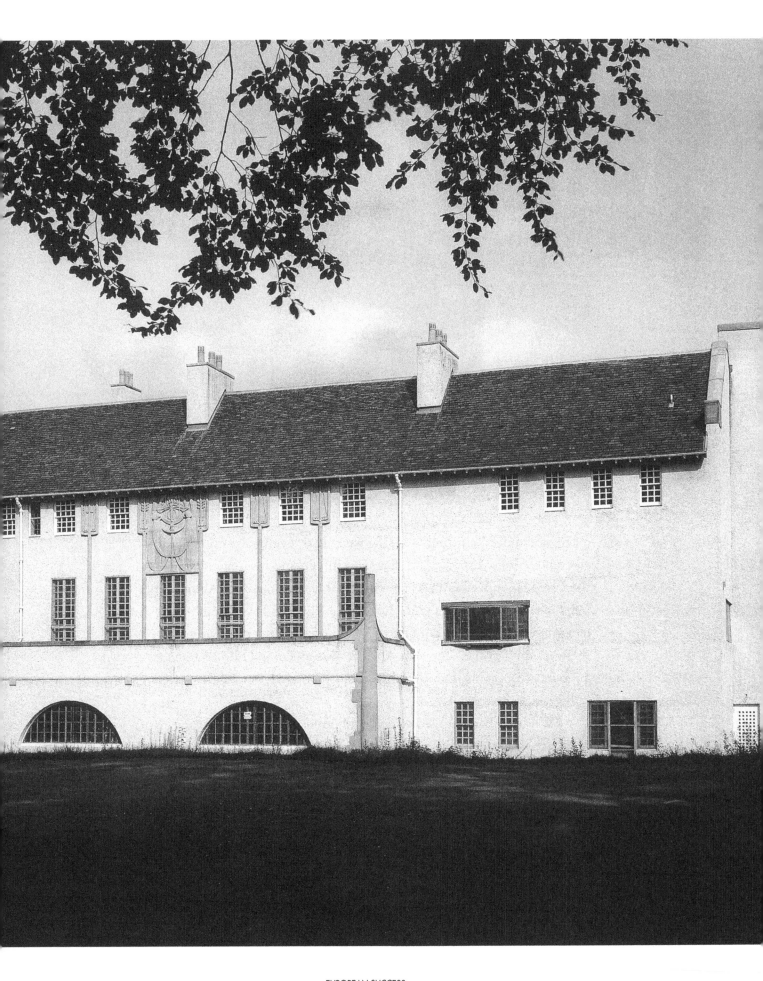

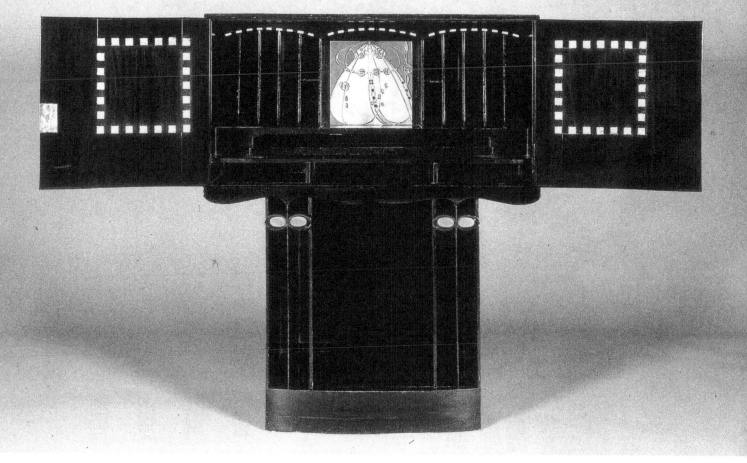

Writing Desk for Hill House.

Mackintosh was a perfectionist, and believed that every item of furniture be created should have not only a physical use, but also an aesthetic purpose. His designs are strikingly indiviual and beautifully made.

made, and indeed nurtured over the past years, eventually cooled. He was an intensely respected artist and architect, and his influence on the European movement was undeniable. He continued to exhibit until 1909, but his last contact with Vienna was likely to have been his meeting with the Werkstatte designer, Eduard Wimmer in Glasgow, as the west wing of the School of Art was nearing completion. Wimmer announced upon his return that the charismatic Mackintosh had been sadly reduced by drink.

While he had enjoyed critical and popular acclaim in Europe, Mackintosh achieved little satisfying recognition in Scotland or in England. He was made a partner in Honeyman and Keppie in 1902, a long-awaited position, and he became a fellow of the Royal Institute of British Architects in 1906 and of the Royal Incorporation of Architects in Scotland in 1908, but he became increasingly disillusioned. Despite a happy domestic life, with a calm, inspiring partner, an idyllic home, two Persian cats and a shared outlook, he began to drink heavily. This drew to a close his fruitful Glasgow years.

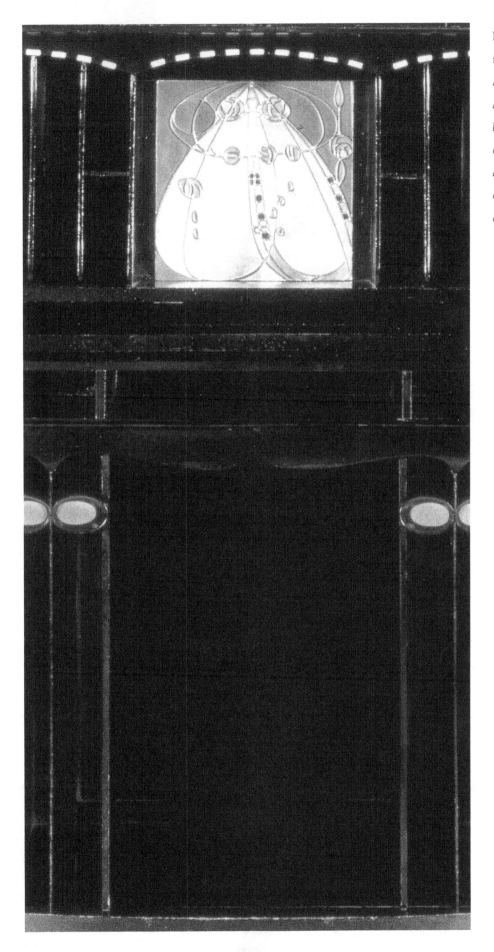

Detail of Writing Desk for Hill House.

Mackintosh used glasswork and designs such as this to break up the natural surface of the furniture. These details brought light and colour to even the most solid of wooden pieces.

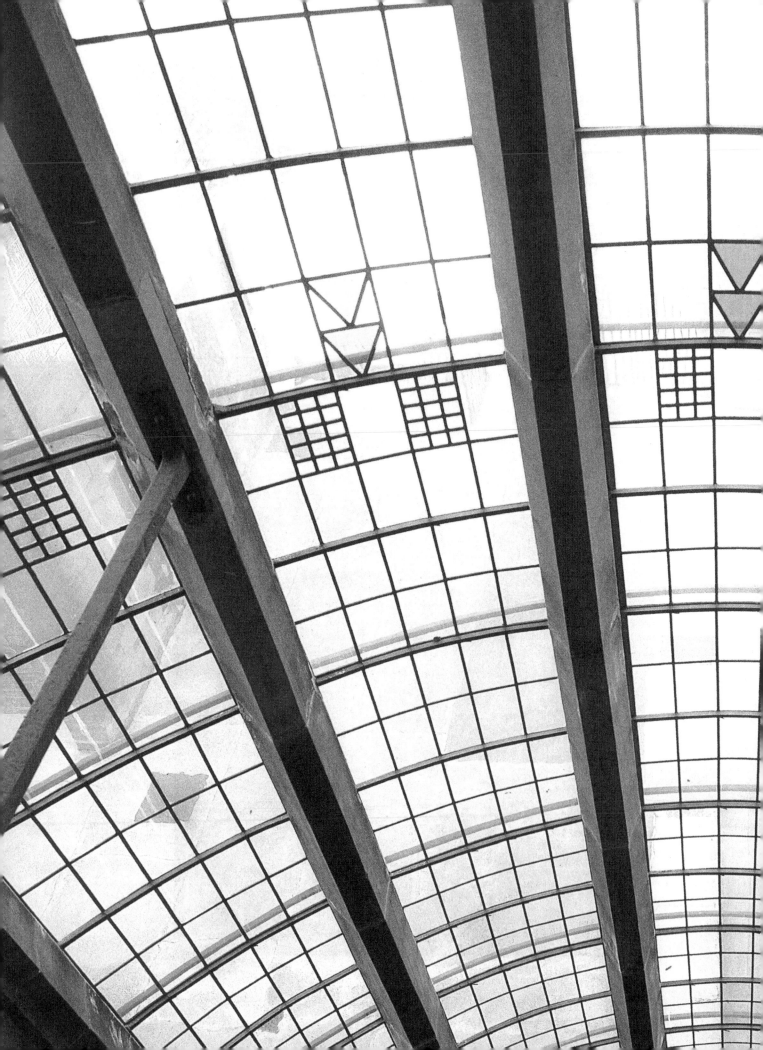

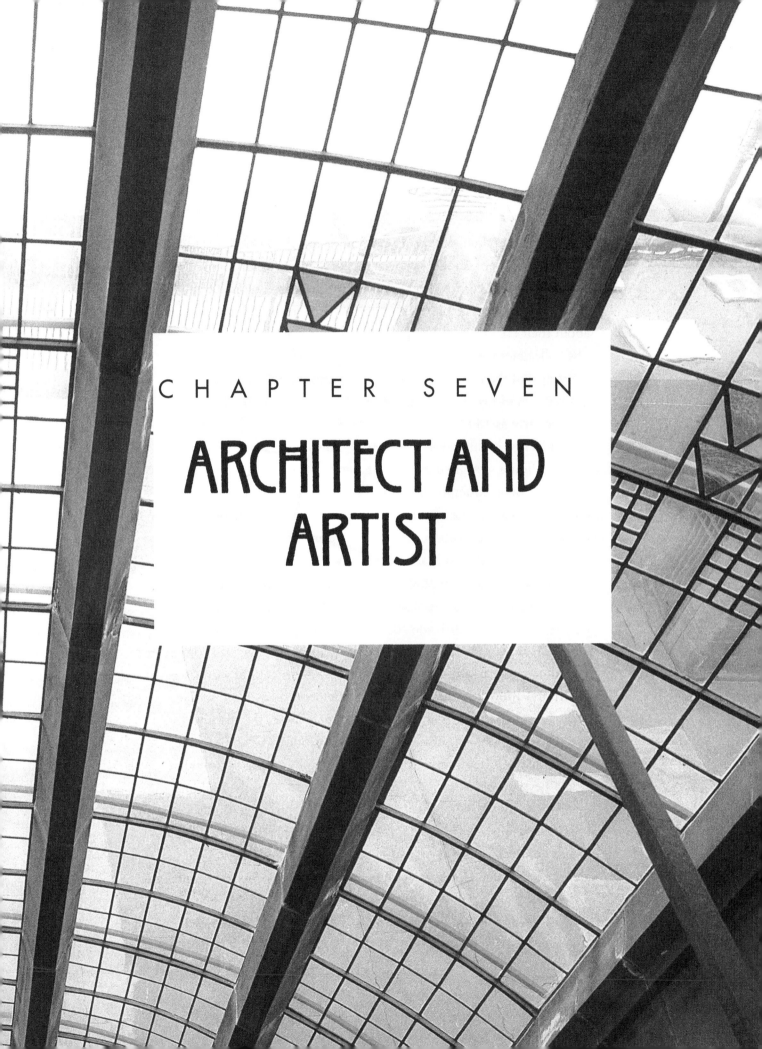

CHAPTER SEVEN

ARCHITECT AND ARTIST

If I were God I would design like Mackintosh.

Robert Mallet-Stevens

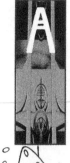

LTHOUGH IT IS HIS design, his unique vision for a complete environment, and his exquisitely original work in textiles, glass, furniture and furnishings that have given Mackintosh his name, it is in the field of architecture that Charles Rennie Mackintosh made his most significant and long-lasting contribution.

Within a ten-year period, from 1896 to 1906, he was established as an important architect, producing buildings that were both highly individual and consciously rooted in the Scottish tradition of the seventeenth and eighteenth centuries. Mackintosh's work came through the offices of Honeyman and Keppie, but there was no doubt about their creator, for his idiosyncratic style was intensely his own. His colleagues were aware of his growing interest and reputation in painting and the applied arts, but his contribution to the company assured him of his place within it, and he began to undertake perspectives as early as 1893.

His first building for Honeyman and Keppie was the *Glasgow Herald* building, designed in 1893. It was a traditional Queen Anne, Scotch Baronial structure, but with an extraordinary tower, which recalled the campanile tower at Siena, which he had sketched on his Italian tour two years earlier. The proportions of its façade were strongly identified with Mackintosh, as well as the series of vertical windows arranged in the tower. The drawing later appeared in *Academy Architecture,* and his ogee roof with the heavy weathervane were noted features that Mackintosh was to use again.

The design for Queen Margaret's Medical College was completed over the next year, and it was the first of his architectural works to incorporate both structural and natural elements as a united whole. Although the design was attributed to John Keppie, the plain walls and the seemingly indiscriminately placed windows relating to the internal uses of the rooms within, were early characteristics of what would become the Mackintosh style. The elevation of the building was dependent upon the uses of the rooms, in keeping with his 'inside to outside' approach. The perspective was published both in *The British Architect* on 10 January 1896, and in *Building News*, which described it as an 'excellent structure, treated with boldness and simplicity and originality in the details'.

A third building, designed in 1895, shows a surer and more

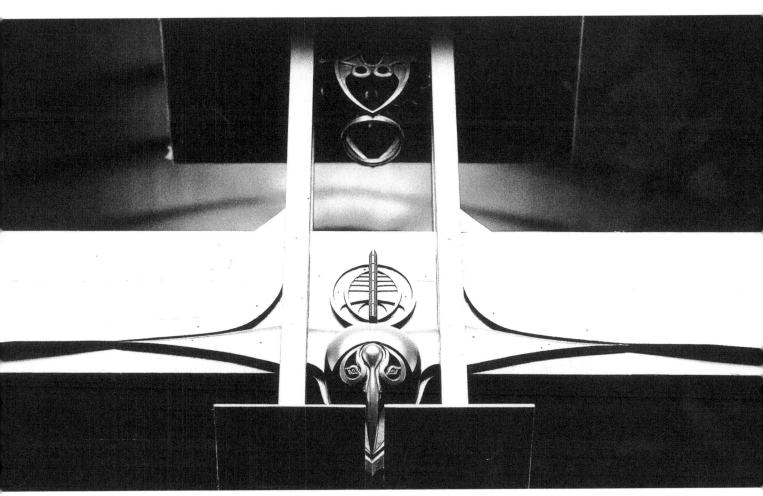

characteristically Mackintosh hand at work: Martyr's Public School. Once again the windows were its crowning glory, with light flowing in from a translucent glass roof. The perspective indicates a building that is Scotch Baronial in design, but with interesting features – a section of roof which projects nearly three feet from the face of the wall, supported by brackets that anticipated the eaves of the Glasgow School of Art. Mackintosh avoided the use of decorative elements, concentrating instead on the structure of the building according to the function of the rooms within.

The following year, 1896, marked the design of the Glasgow School of Art (see page 34), undoubtedly one of Mackintosh's greatest achievements. Within the period of time that the School was designed and built, Mackintosh also took on a number of other commissions, including The Queen's Cross Church, which was built between 1897 and 1899. The church is traditional in approach, but Mackintosh incorporated a number of modern details, including using metal structural supports in a decorative manner, and adorning the pulpit with carved floral motifs from The Glasgow Four. Mackintosh's decision to leave the iron exposed was bold, and consistent with his determination to

Detail of a Beam Above the Altar in the Queen's Cross Church.

The ironwork in the Queen's Cross church was left exposed, and Mackintosh used the metal structures to decorative purpose, creating a modern feel that contrasted with the traditional elements of the church.

combine traditional elements with industrial materials. The ironwork throughout the rest of the church, particularly in the railings, emphasizes this dichotomy, and is full of pictorial allusions. David Brett, in C. R. *Mackintosh: The Poetics of Workmanship*, wrote, '… ironwork can be seen to be setting forth its own craft: in the railing of the Queen's Cross Church there is a form that, reminiscent of the 'head' of the immured figure in The Tree of Influence, emblemizes the blacksmith's tongs. Here it is as if the iron has become conscious of itself as having been wrought. Ironwork becomes the bearer of wit; it is the most playful and self-allusive element.'

The *Daily Record* building was Mackintosh's next major commission, and it was completed in 1901, the year of Glasgow's International Exhibition. The location for the building was dark and constrained, and Mackintosh was challenged to produce a building that was both commanding and somehow light. The strong verticals of the resulting building are echoes of his earlier graphic work, and on the façade he has used white ceramic tile to the fourth floor, where it changes to sandstone. There is a strong upward movement, defined by the occasional projecting brick. It is a symmetrical pattern, and any external decoration was concentrated around the windows and doors.

As the first stage of the School of Art building was completed, towards the end of the nineteenth century, Mackintosh received his first independent commission. The businessman and art collector, William Davidson, asked Mackintosh to work on Windyhill, his family house at Kilmacolm. The construction of the house took place between 1900 and 1901, and is largely consistent with Mackintosh's nationalist ethic. By using simple massing, and carefully arranging the shapes and position of openings in the robust walls, he produced a building that was derived from the vernacular expressed in the traditional Scottish farmhouse, but he simplified it in order to achieve a more modern feel. There is a firm angularity to the design, and a preoccupation with elevations which were not confirmed until the internal arrangements had been submitted and approved. This was consistent with Mackintosh's idea that a building should fulfil the purpose for which it was designed and, in the architect's mind, the use of the building was much more important to its overall structure than symmetry.

The Windyhill interior was Mackintosh's first real opportunity to amalgamate design and art within his own structure, and the result is extraordinarily coherent: the square windows are echoed in the timbered divides within the rooms, and in the light fittings themselves, the overall effect is one of spartan light and of simple elegance. This was the prototype for the work that was to come in Hill House, his next commission.

Hill House was commissioned by Walter Blackie, a Glasgow Publisher who wanted to create a new home for himself at Helensburgh, to the west of Glasgow. The designs were completed in 1902, and once again, Mackintosh had worked from the inside out. He spent a great deal of time with the Blackie family, in order to assess their needs, and then supplied designs of the inside only. Blackie himself recalled, 'Not until we had dccidcd on these inside arrangements did he submit drawings of the elevations.'

The finished designs were, unexpectedly, exactly what Blackie had hoped for and the building itself was one of the most important and elegant domestic homes created anywhere in Britain. Like Windyhill and the School of Art, the external walls were 'harled' to provide an impression of the Scottish vernacular tradition, but once again, there is a decided Japanese influence in the contrast between interior and exterior. While the exterior is sturdily Scottish, the interior is redolent of Oriental themes, which are integrated into his overall concept. There are 58 windows in Hill House, based on about 40

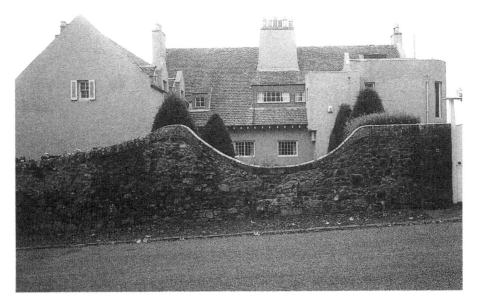

Windyhill, Kilmacolm.
The exterior of Windyhill was designed in the style of a traditional Scottish farmhouse. The house was created, however, as a holistic entity and the elevations were not completed until the plans for the interior had been approved.

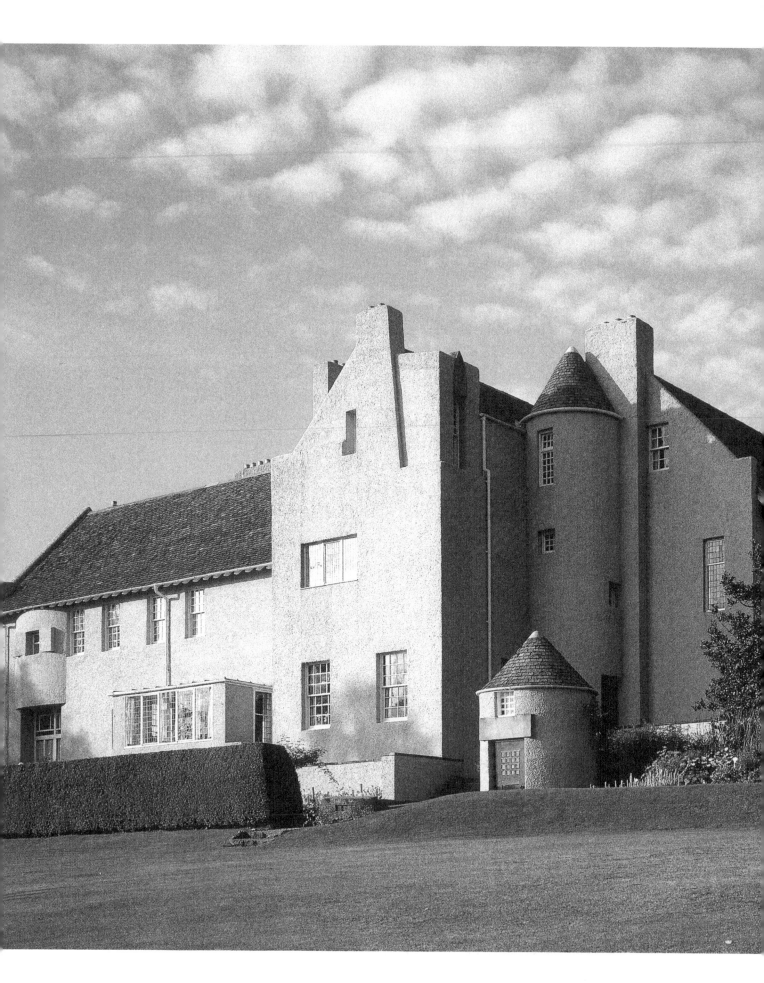

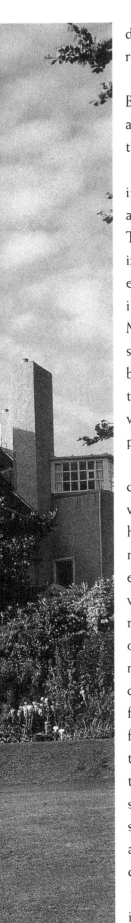

different designs, and while the size is largely consistent, the square or rectangular shape of the panes are ever-changing.

The interior was compromized to a certain extent because Blackie could not afford to decorate and furnish the whole house according to Mackintosh's designs, so the efforts were concentrated on the library, hall, principal bedroom and drawing room.

The library is traditionally masculine, panelled in dark wood inlaid with squares of coloured glass. The tall moulding curves in the almost completely rectilinear room, provide freedom of movement. The hall is also accented with the same dark framing that characterized Windyhill, but the broad uprights are inlaid with purple-enamelled glass and the wall between is stencilled with organic motifs in shades of blue, pink and green. The drawing room is one of Mackintosh's 'white rooms', where white walls are decorated with stencilled roses and trellis patterns in pink, grey and green accented by silver paper. The light pours in through a low-ceilinged bay window, and there is a large fireplace in the corner.

TWO BLACK LADDERBACK CHAIRS, A JUXTAPOSITION OF MASCULINITY WITH EXQUISITE FEMININITY

The framing of the hall is carried up into the apsidal tower, where the principal bedroom is housed. The room is at once feminine and delicate, hung with embroidered panels of dreaming women. The walls are a soft cream, with a delicate row of stencilled, olive green and pink roses running round the room. In strong contrast to the subtle, sensuous atmosphere of the bedroom are two black ladderback chairs, a juxtaposition of masculinity with exquisite femininity. The tops of the chairs are chequered, a theme which is carried throughout the house in the form of squares – coloured, and black and white, on the carpets, the furniture and the walls. Coloured light comes through the squares in the doors and uprights, and purple and blue radiate from the glass in the masculine rooms, while pink and white shimmer in the feminine spaces. Alan Crawford writes: ' ... they are not intrusive; by now the square was less a motif in Mackintosh's hands than a method of articulating surfaces and spaces. From about 1900 one can feel it challenging the curves which characterized his mouldings of the 1890s and the organic ornament of the early 1900s. The Hill House is a point of transition.'

Hill House,
Helensburgh.
When planning houses such
as Windyhill or Hill
House, Mackintosh worked
closely with the owners to
assess their requirements and
tastes and to incorporate
these into both the interior
and exterior of the designs.

Drawing Room at
Hill House.

The Drawing Room at Hill
House is a traditionally
light 'feminine' room,
coloured in white, pink, grey
and green, with characteristic
Mackintosh rose stencils
and trellis patterns

As the Blackies moved into Hill House in 1904, Mackintosh was busily preparing designs for another house, Hous'hill, in the outskirts of Glasgow. He was required only to produce an interior for the seventeenth-century mansion, whose tenants were Major John Cochrane and his wife, Catherine Cranston. It was an important achievement, and will be documented in detail in the following chapter.

Upon completing the building of Hill House in 1904, Mackintosh had already designed and implemented Miss Cranston's Willow Tea Rooms, and he continued to supply furniture for Hill House, and for the School of Art over the next year. Hous'hill was underway, while Mackintosh worked on a number of smaller commissions. Between 1904 and 1906, he created the Scotland Street School, a beautiful building created from red sandstone and accented by two circular staircase towers with conical roofs. Once again, Mackintosh juxtaposed the castle form with the free style, but instead of his traditional use of arrow-slit windows, he chose to use a curved, glass screen that runs up four floors of the building. The two towers represent the separation of the sexes, and between the towers he created a small, surprisingly indulgent entrance for the infants.

Characteristically, there is a liberal use of symbolic ironwork, and the sandstone façade is broken by squares of coloured glass and a highly stylized organic motif. The detailing is original and much more complex than his previous work. He decorated the stonework around the top of the main tower windows with little peaked and winged motifs, the top of the upper windows are headed by a band of vertical mouldings on which the winged motif is dispersed. Alan Crawford writes: 'After several years with the harled Scottish vernacular, which has few mouldings and moves from wall to window, solid to void, in an instant, Mackintosh returned to stone and a public building, and created mouldings which give life to the stone and make a transition between wall and window. At the back, the stylized central images are a Scottish thistle and a Tree of Life, composed of Viennese-inspired squares and triangles.'

In 1906, the Mackintoshes moved to a house in Florentine Terrace, and once again they created together an aesthetic environment in which their artistic spirits were able to soar. Alan Crawford spoke to Mary Sturrock, Francis Newbery's youngest daughter, who recalled 'this interior and that of Florentine Terrace ... [as] a single happy image. The house was always so pretty and fresh. But what seems to come across is that they were so awfully nice. A bright red glowing

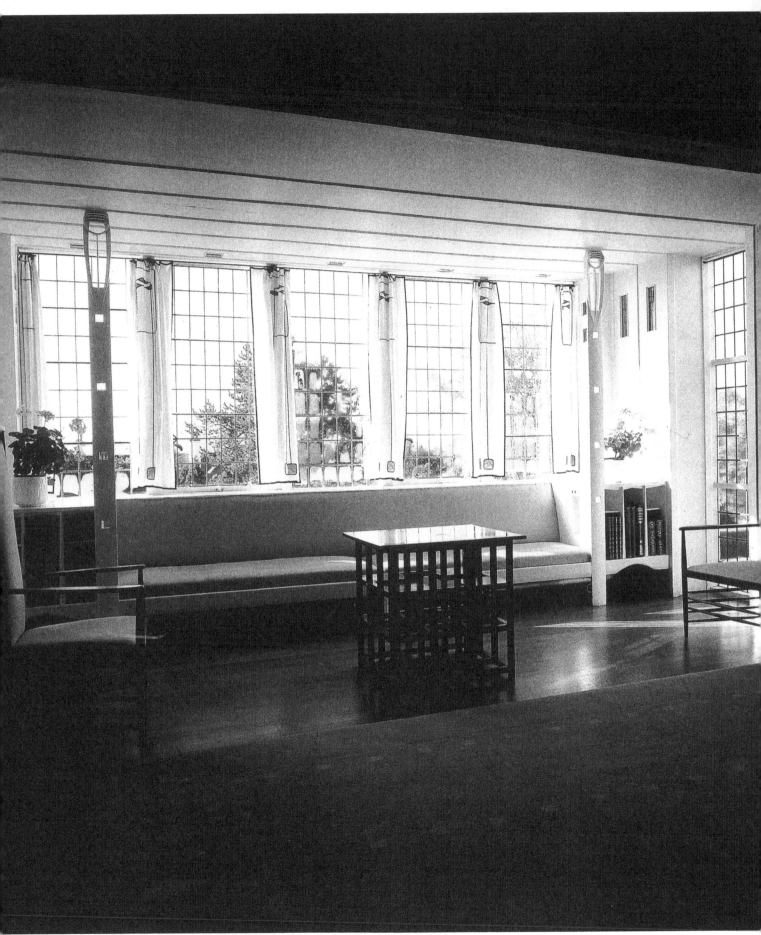

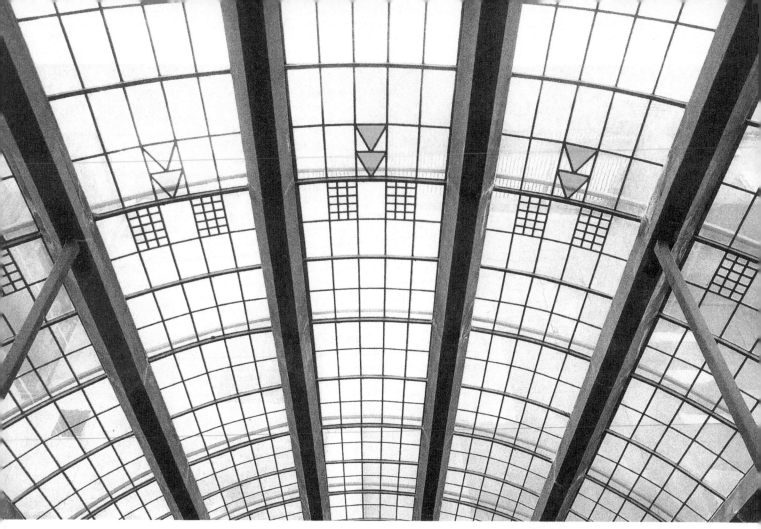

fire, the right sort of cake, a nice tea, and kind hearts – and a lot of fun.'

These prolific years were marked by a buzz of activity, and it hardly seems possible that Mackintosh was able to sustain the pace. He continued to supply furniture for Hous'hill until 1909, and worked on furnishings for the Holy Trinity Church, Bridge of Allan; a dining room for the exhibition by A. S. Ball in Berlin; the eastern extension of the School of Art; the work on his own home, Florentine Terrace; the Dutch Kitchen at the Argyle Street Tea Rooms; the Scotland Street School; and the Auchinibert and Mosside houses (both unassuming homes for private clients) throughout 1906.

But the completion of the western wing of the School of Art marked the high point of Mackintosh's architectural career, and a steady decline in commissions followed. The next four and a half years were largely empty, with Mackintosh dealing with only six new projects. He was always an opinionated man and a perfectionist; difficult to work with and ruthlessly making change after change in his pursuit of that perfection. Previous clients had accepted Mackintosh's exacting standards and high-handed approach because of his singular devotion to his work and his undoubted talents. But eventually people began to object to such treatment, and when Mackintosh began to drink heavily, they threatened to take their business elsewhere. Mackintosh became unreliable, and the firm, of which he was now a partner, began to suffer serious financial difficulties.

Mackintosh started to suffer from depression, and the alcohol became a solace for the misery of the years leading up to the First World War. Nikolaus Pevsner wrote: 'During his best years … he sometimes arrived at the office in the evening with piles of sheets of paper, ready to fill them during the night either with sketches or large-scale details drawn with the greatest possible accuracy. In the morning they would find him exhausted and drunk, and the sheets of paper covered with drawings so perfect they might have been jewels'.

But Mackintosh could not sustain this demanding attempt to continue creating, and after an argument over a local competition, he resigned from Honeyman and Keppie, and the partnership of Honeyman, Keppie and Mackintosh was formally dissolved in June 1914.

For some months, Mackintosh worked from the practice's old premises at 140 Bath Street, and later from home, but his vision of creating a new art in Glasgow, based on a renaissance of Scottish architecture had been shattered, and his spirit all but died. In 1914, the Mackintoshes closed their home, and moved from Glasgow, waving a final farewell to Mackintosh's hopes and ambitions and, sadly, his architectural career.

Interior of the Stair Tower at the Scotland Street School.
The Scotland Street School is characterized by two circular staircase towers, with curved glass screens that run up four floors of the building. Here again, Mackintosh makes use of glass to allow maximum natural light into the building.

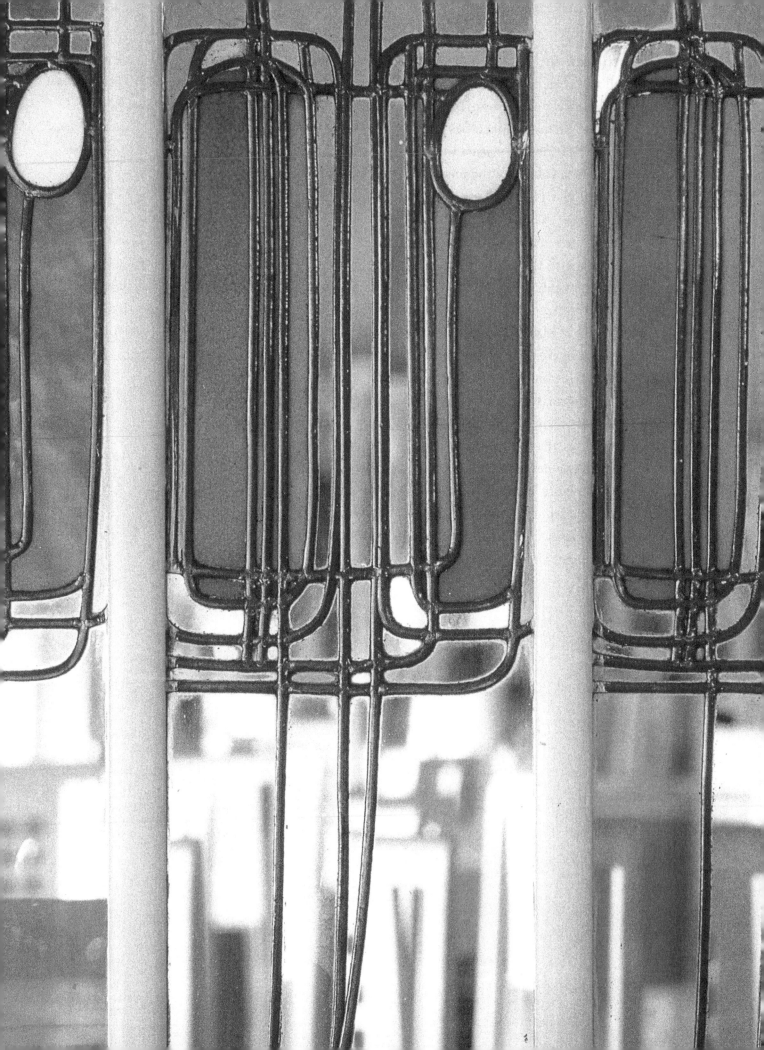

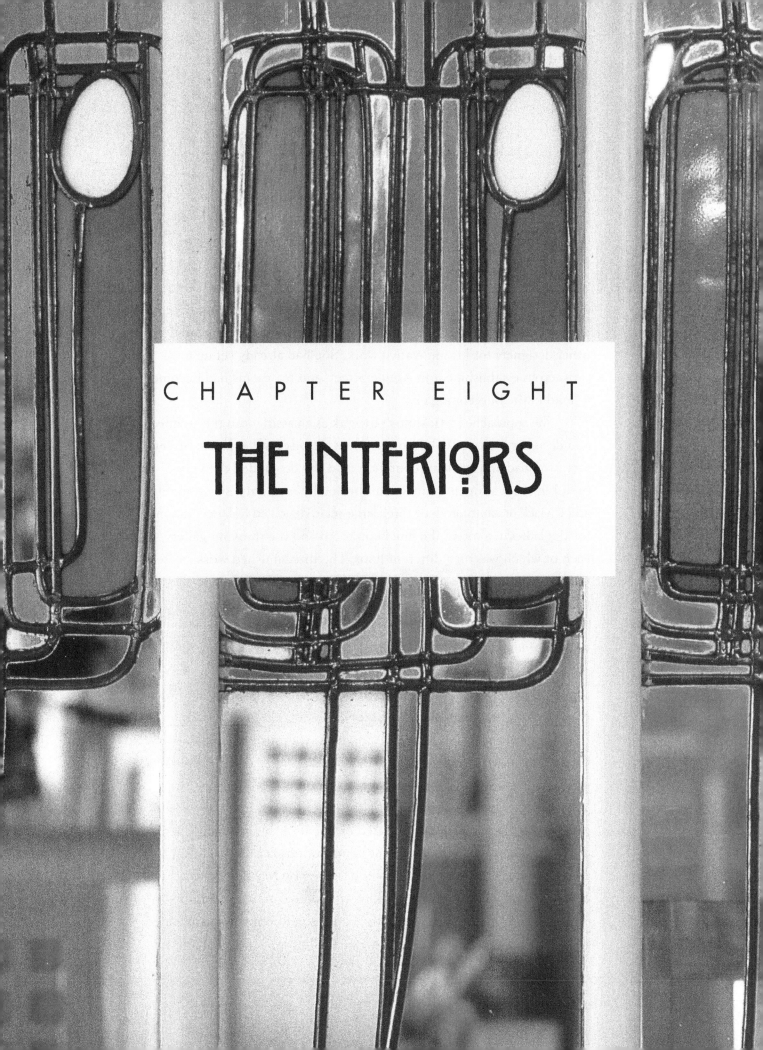

CHAPTER EIGHT

THE INTERIORS

... the room as work of art, as a unified organic whole, embracing colour, form and atmosphere ... starting from this notion they develop not only the room, but the whole house, the sole purpose of the exterior of which is to enclose the rooms.

Hermann Muthesius, writing of The Four's work

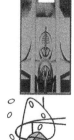

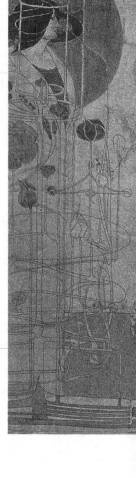

EARLIER ON IN HIS career, in 1896, Mackintosh had met a woman who was to exert an enormous influence on his professional life. She was Miss Catherine (Kate) Cranston, a local businesswoman with a firm belief in Temperance. She came up with the idea for a series of 'art tea rooms', which would help to rid her native city of the 'demon drink'. Kate Cranston was an ideal woman to work with, being both artistic, clever and determined, and she chose Mackintosh from countless other designers for his innovative work. She had already set up a prosperous establishment in Argyle Street, and tea rooms had become a trend in the burgeoning city.

She approached Mackintosh to work as an assistant to the architect and designer George Walton on her new premises in Buchanan Street. Cranston had an excellent reputation, and she demanded the very best, but she was open-minded and thrilled by creativity in action. She asked Mackintosh to produce three large-scale stencilled wall decorations for the ladies' tea room, the luncheon room and the smoking gallery, each of which was on a different floor. The three finished works were intended to symbolize the transition from earth to heaven, and they were so controversial that curious patrons flooded in, making the rooms an instant success. The murals were painted directly on the walls, and featured elongated women, redolent of the Glasgow Style, interwoven with organic forms, tendrils, leaves and shoots. The repeating pattern was broken by stylized trees, once again exhibiting a pantheistic Celtic influence on his work.

The success of the tea rooms forged a relationship between Cranston and Mackintosh. In 1987, she hired him again, this time in a more involved role, for the design of her Argyle Street Tea Rooms. Walton was responsible for creating the space, marked by screens and panels, and Mackintosh concentrated on the furnishings. Alan Jones describes the most significant of his contributions, a high-backed chair: 'Among the furniture is a chair designed by Mackintosh that is one of the most unforgettably striking silhouettes in the history of design, a high-backed chair from the Luncheon Room, the exaggerated vertical stress and wide oval panel with cut-through stylized flying

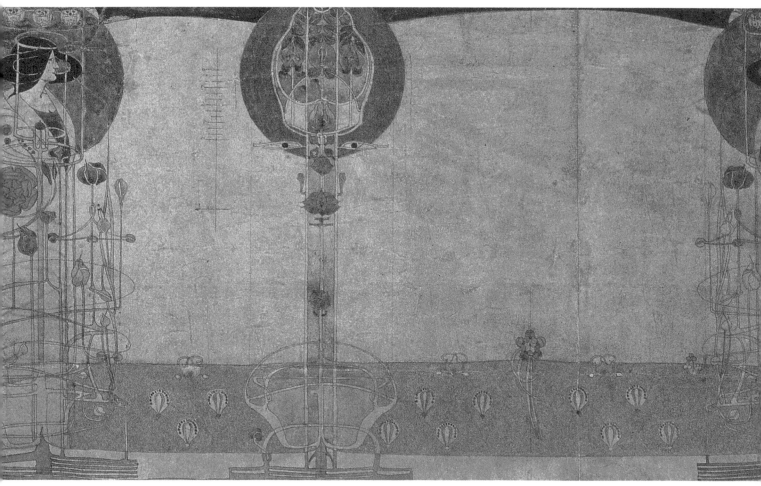

bird giving it a significant presence in the room, whether occupied or not. When seated in these chairs at a table in the busy restaurant, one felt that they created a light, open screen around the table, to make a room within a room.'

The Argyle Street Tea Rooms were as successful as their predecessors, and Mackintosh's name became synonymous with that of Kate Cranston. In 1900 he was asked to redesign both the furniture and the interiors of the Ingram Street Tea Rooms, originally designed by the architect Kesson Whyte, and decorated by two design partnerships. The brief was tighter than his previous commissions, and he was asked to provide a visual unity between the rooms. He opened up the walls and created a series of interconnected rooms. Glorying in the possibilities of definition by opposites, he created a white ladies lunch room, filled with light from the large windows in contrast with a dark, panelled billiard room below. The ladies lunch room had screened-off tables, and panelling to a height of about ten feet. The cornice of the panelling ran across the front of the windows as in the Mackintoshes' home at Mains Street. The frieze was filled with gesso panels, one by Margaret and the other by Mackintosh. The panels were created on rough material,

Mural for the Buchanan Street Tea Rooms.

The Tea Rooms in Buchanan Street were the first Mackintosh worked on. Murals such as this one were painted on the walls, and featured the elongated women and organic images characteristic of the Glasgow Style.

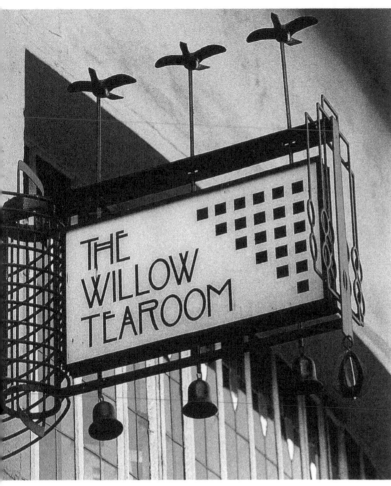

Sign for the Willow
Tea Rooms.

The chequerboard pattern
featured here was a motif
that was repeated not only
throughout the interior of the
Tea Rooms, but was also
painted up the side of the
building to make
the house stand out.

covered with coloured gesso, with string to define figures and trees. Coloured glass, beads and metal were then applied.

The Cloister Room was originally designed around the existing plasterwork, but this was later redesigned with a lower vaulted ceiling and light panelling. The Chinese Room, designed several years later, was Mackintosh's *pièce de résistance*, featuring a series of latticework screens in bright turquoise and jewel-like colours, which was offset by black lacquered furniture and a dark ceiling.

The Willow Tea Rooms were created over the years 1903 and 1904, and Kate Cranston anticipated, quite rightly, that they would become her showpieces. For the first time, Mackintosh was given complete control over the building and interior work, and although the building already existed, it was a largely gutted terraced house which Mackintosh was able to recreate to his own design. He painted the façade of the building white, and ran a chequerboard pattern up the edge of the building to set it out from the neighbouring houses. The interior, from the signboards and the menus to the furniture and the light fittings, were designed as complete works of art. With Margaret's assistance, Mackintosh designed the wall decorations, the furniture, the carpets and even decided upon the appropriate cutlery and dress for the staff members.

An exquisite chandelier in the form of a hanging basket of flowers lit up the centre of the main dining room. For the ground floor, Mackintosh designed the 'Willow Tea Room chair', essentially a stylized interpretation of the willow tree, which was to act both as a chair and a form of space division within the rooms. The use of colour was restrained, and on the upper floor of the Willow Tea Rooms, Mackintosh used a mainly black and white theme, suggesting a Japanese influence. Here, a large proportion of the roof was removed to illuminate the room, and the ceiling was replaced with a drape of muslin.

On the first floor near the front of the building is the heart of the tea rooms, the 'Room De Luxe'. The interior was partly mirrored, and accented with silver, grey and pink. Resplendent stained-glass doors were set in the entrance, and the walls were decorated with Mackintosh's now familiar rose motif, and other natural forms.

The decorative scheme of the Willow Tea Room was based mainly on the willow-tree form, which culminated in a gesso panel produced by Margaret, and inspired by Rossetti's sonnet, 'O ye, all ye that walk in the willow wood.'

The pierced pattern of the chair backs was echoed in the soft grey carpet which was lined and patterned in squares. A balcony was bordered with wrought iron balustrades and the front section of the restaurant was lined with a white plaster wall frieze. Bright colours were used only sparingly, and Mackintosh used light and dark to delineate the space.

Over the next decade, Mackintosh was to revise his designs for Cranston's tea rooms altering various rooms and experimenting with more vibrant colours – reds and blues, as opposed to his traditional soft greys, purples and pinks. He went on to create the Dutch Kitchen and the Dug-Out for Cranston, and they remained firm friends, with Mackintosh eventually creating her domestic interiors at Hous'hill in 1904.

Windyhill and Hill House offered Mackintosh the opportunity to create an integrated external and internal design, and these interiors are, even today, a remarkable achievement. He used stencils throughout in order to establish a harmonious scheme within an interior and at Hill House, a simple stencilled rose pattern in soft green and pink was repeated around the room and echoed in the stencilled pattern of the window-seat upholstery and the gesso panel and embroidered decoration created by Margaret. In the hallway of Hill House, Mackintosh's chequerboard squares are softened by curves and tendrils, in purple, blue, pink and green which are repeated in the carpets.

Mackintosh used the fireplace as a symbol, creating simple designs, usually with plain surrounds and coloured glass or tiles inset for effect. He used light in an extraordinarily effective way, manipulating both artificial and natural light to achieve various effects. He created rooms which could be adapted to a variety of functions. At Hill House, he created a room which could be used both as a music room and a drawing room, according to the seasons. In winter, a couch was

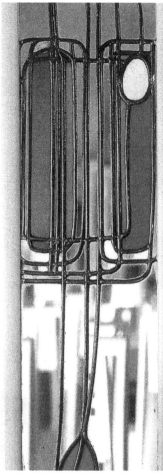

Glass Panel from the Willow Tea Rooms.

The silver, grey, white and pink used in the glass inset here were the colours that characterized the 'Room De Luxe'. Stained glass was also used in the doors and windows of the Tea Rooms.

drawn towards the fireplace to create an enclosed space, while summer evenings could be spent in the bay windows, which were designed to house the piano and window seat.

Alan Jackson described the unique interior at Hill House: 'The Hill House was not just a sequence of rooms; it is a home whose largest meanings and smallest details were transformed by the Mackintoshes' art ... [it is] full of alternations and gradations of light which reinforce the masculine/feminine scheme of meanings: gloom in the vestibule, half-light in the hall, bright light beckoning us on the stairs and welcoming us in the drawing room and bedroom ... when the sun comes out, the whole house responds to it ...'

Both Windyhill and Hill House were rich with images of nature, which drew visitors in from the outside in a simple, elegant movement, and which were repeated throughout in both furniture and decoration. These houses were the realization of Mackintosh's holistic vision, and each one has a unique and repetitive imagery used consistently within and upon its walls.

WHEN THE SUN COMES OUT, THE WHOLE HOUSE RESPONDS

Hous'hill, Kate Cranston's home, was to present a challenge, for he was to work on the interiors alone. Mackintosh chose to design a simple, intelligent interior, and he avoided the decorative tension of Hill House and Windyhill. In the dining room, a frieze rail circled the room, crossing the windows, with box-like light fittings hanging over the table. Cranston and her husband had a great deal of good, solid furniture, and Mackintosh worked his designs to complement these traditional pieces. The walls were stencilled with repeating patterns in two parts, with oblongs and rectangles topped by clusters of flowers.

In the drawing room, he created a spectacular curved, open screen comprised of white-painted fins, this allowed a place for a piano which was to be the focus of the room. He placed chairs in front of the screen in an opposing arch, and ran stretchers along the floor. The circular screen was matched by the large bay window, and a top rail formed a complete circle, resting on the fitted seats and running across the spaces in between.

Two bedrooms were created and furnished in 1904. The Blue Bedroom contained dark-stained furniture, and the White Bedroom was in stark contrast accented by only small squares of colour. The

Bedroom at

78 Derngate.

Derngate was Mackintosh's final interior, and is perhaps his most striking. Here he employed bold primary colours and geometric shapes, lacking the usual natural association of his work.

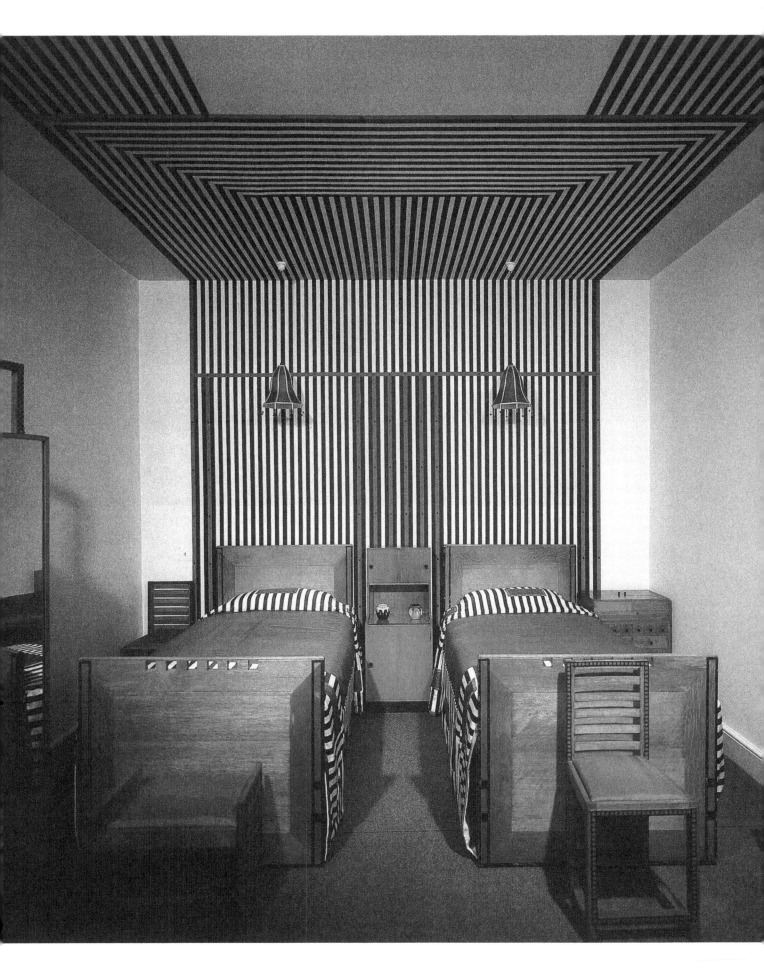

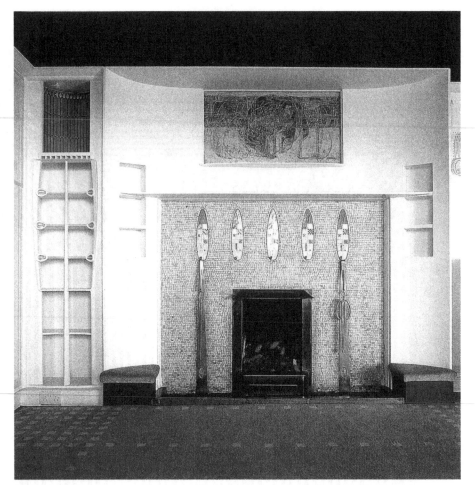

White Bedroom was fitted with a short border of stencilled patterns which wove around the room, decorated with a simple, repetitive motif.

The most important aspect of Hous'hill is the change it marked in Mackintosh's work. His interior lacked the vibrant influence of the natural world, and his motif, repeated throughout, was the square, which certainly had no real natural associations. The rooms lack his previous sensuality, perhaps most evident in his avoidance of fecund natural symbols, and the sense of spiritual integration is more clinical, and less welcoming. Nevertheless, the house suited Cranston and her husband and it is a good example of Mackintosh's use of functional space.

Mackintosh's final interior of note is 78 Derngate, Northampton, which he created in 1916, after he had left Glasgow. The interiors were commissioned by W. J. Bassett-Lowke, and they were some of the most imaginative and ingenious designs ever produced. The furniture was comprised of simple, bold, black pieces accented with small chips of inlaid plastic. The overwhelming emphasis is on black, and there is a rigid geometrication using wallpapers rather than stencils. Grid patterns, hard triangles, strong lines are confidently presented in a shocking combination of primary colours that stand starkly in contrast to the all-black furniture. While Hous'hill marked the transition between the natural and the geometric, Derngate is completely devoid of any natural associations, anticipating the Art Deco movement with its broad, bold strokes of colour and geometry.

Bassett-Lowke was delighted with the end result, which he described as 'distinctly futuristic', and it was published in *Ideal Home* in 1920, although the magazine failed to note Mackintosh's role in creating it.

Mackintosh's interiors seemed to follow a specific pattern, in that a style was developed in a domestic setting and then repeated for tea rooms and various exhibitions. For many reasons, the interiors – particularly the individual pieces of furniture and decorations – worked less effectively in a more clinical environment, probably because they were produced as part of a whole, a holistic unit, and out of that space, they lacked the embracing spirit.

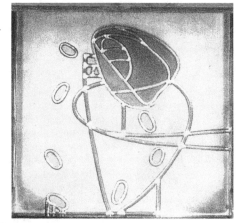

Desk for Hous'hill.
The furniture Mackintosh made for Hous'hill, the Cranston's home, was designed to complement the traditional furniture which they already owned, yet it still carries the Mackintosh style.

His interiors are appreciated far more today than they were during Mackintosh's lifetime, and they provoked much more controversy than approval, although the domestic interiors were created with the in-habitants in mind and therefore could not fail to please. Alistair Duncan, in *Art Nouveau*, wrote: 'Today, as one examines Mackintosh's sur-viving interiors, it is hard to comprehend the genuine outrage they aroused at the time. Certainly some of his decorative motifs can be considered weird or disquieting, particularly the ghost-like visions of attenuated young women ... but the crisp verticality and the spatial articulation of his interiors stood in stark refutation of the curved con-tours and *entrelacs* prevalent on the Continent and for this he seems never to have received the credit he deserved.'

Today, the Mackintosh designs are synonymous with Glasgow, and with the Scottish spirit – natural and traditional elements com-plementing a new, free style. His holism is today universally admired and much emulated, but the recognition came too late.

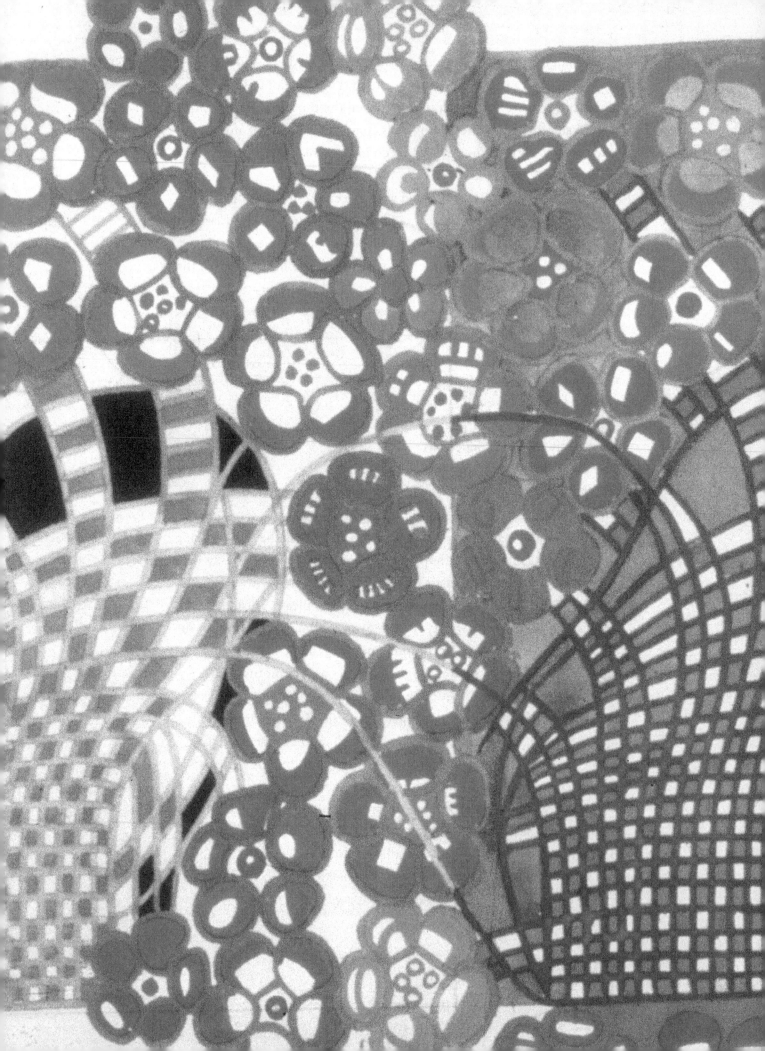

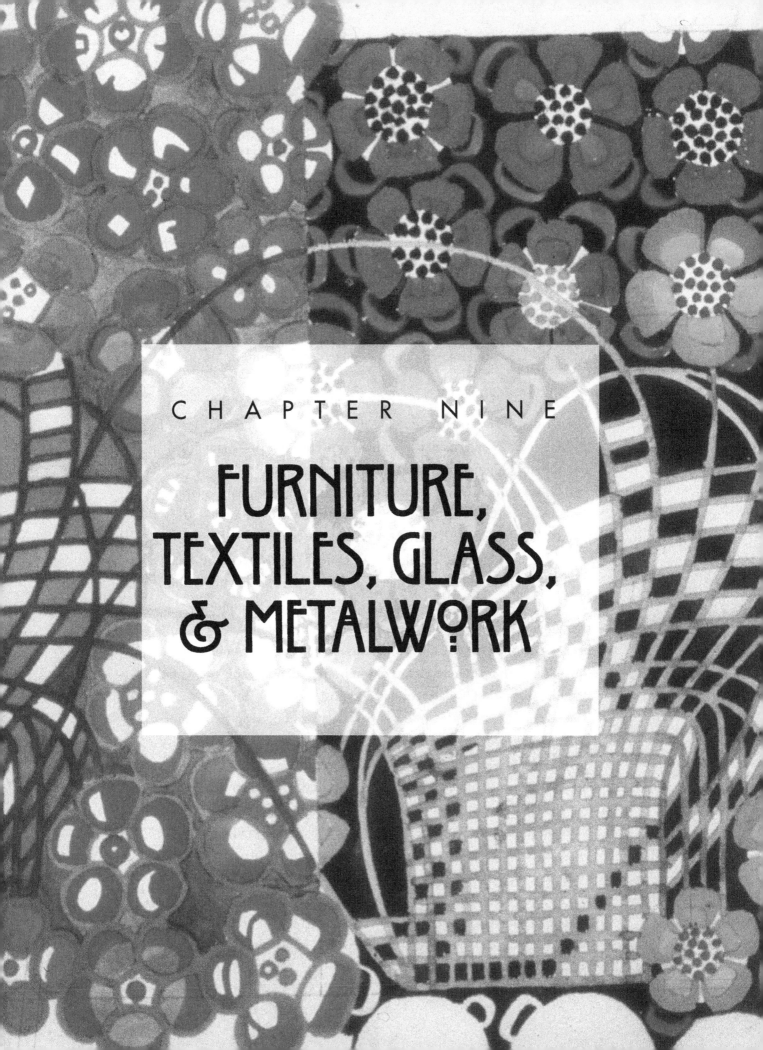

CHAPTER NINE

FURNITURE, TEXTILES, GLASS, & METALWORK

The creative genius of Mackintosh found an expression not only in pure architecture but also in painting and in design of industrial fabrics and furniture and the collection now brought together contains exhibits of extraordinary beauty and originality in all these spheres of art.

Glasgow Herald, 1933

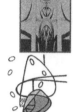

T IS IRONIC that Mackintosh's influential architectural designs were largely unrecognized by his contemporaries. It was as a designer of interiors and furniture that he gained the greatest renown in his own lifetime, and yet today those works are seen as complements and accents to the whole of his architectural creations. Much of his work in the applied arts has been destroyed, or was damaged in its natural life, and only a small percentage of the many items still exist today.

Mackintosh designed over 400 pieces of furniture in his lifetime. He worked mainly in wood, his favourite being oak which he customarily varnished and then, later in his career, painted white and then black. The furniture was designed to delineate space, to accentuate the features of the buildings and recreate them within. Through this Mackintosh was able to refine his stylistic vocabulary.

Mackintosh's chairs were a focus in many rooms, particularly in the Glasgow Tea Rooms, and in most cases they were simple, unadorned pieces which were created to form a part of an overall design. Their simplicity recalls the Arts and Crafts Movement, but their lack of functionality (they were liable to be broken when sat in) and comfort, and their role as 'art' and as decorative elements sets them apart. Fiona and Isla Hackney wrote: 'The theme of the high-backed chair developed far beyond functional needs, becoming a vehicle for Mackintosh's particular brand of symbolism. Echoing the attenuated, heraldic shapes in his watercolours and poster designs, the high-backed chairs for Argyle Street [in particular] can be seen to resemble stylized tree forms, symbols expressive of the upward, surging vitality of so much of Mackintosh's work ... '

Mackintosh and Margaret worked together on their interiors, and the lavish use of symbols – particularly that of the rose – was likely Margaret's romantic influence. But it is this symbolic imagery which provided their furniture with a unique dimension, controlling an atmosphere through a judicious use of interactive and repetitive images. The subtle combinations of colours and shapes would be echoed in shutters, mirrors, friezes and glass.

Mackintosh enjoyed working in wood, but in the early years he

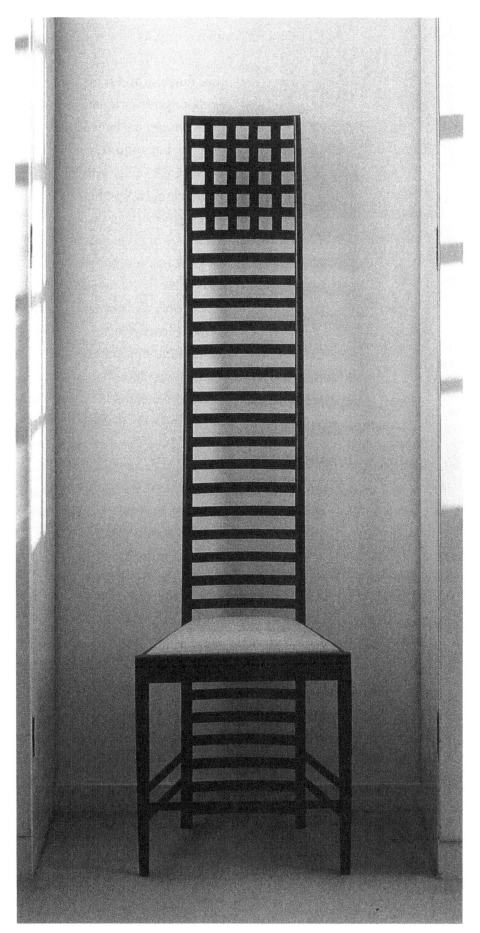

Ladderback Chair.

The ladderback chair has become one of Mackintosh's most recognized styles. When grouped around a table, these were intended to enclose both the table and the guests in a surround of uprights, enhancing the dining experience.

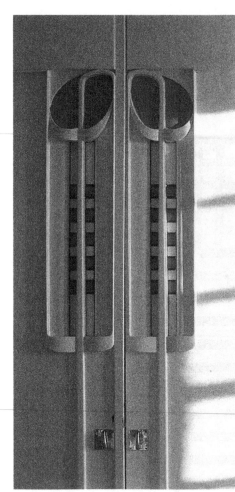

liked to control it by painting it
and altering its face with decoration. His low-backed chairs were
more reliable, and they anticipated
the more geometric imagery that
characterized his later work. Eventually, he began to rely more on
his simple designs, with an
emphasis on exposed grain,
plain surfaces and a distinct
absence of organic motifs. His
work became less curved, less
redolent of Art Nouveau, and
more simple and certainly sophisticated. He used lattice work to
lighten heavy pieces and to
emphasize simple shapes.

Mackintosh's glass work was
used both to break up the natural
surface of the furniture, adding
light to the most solid of pieces,
and it was also used to draw together colour themes within an interior.
Glass was inserted into walls, doors, shutters, fireplaces, panels and in
the light fittings, which glowed with vibrant splashes of colour. He
used panels of leaded glass in furniture and in pendants, and hung it
around and across fireplaces – particularly the hearth at Hill House,
which had a surround of thick plate-glass set horizontally in order to
cast a warm, green glow across the room.

The Room De Luxe in the Willow Tea Rooms formed an elaborate
and inventive part of his *oeuvre*, in which stained glass doors in vibrant
colours opened into a room lined with mirrored panels inlaid with tiny
pieces of enamel. He used glass to add light and to cast colour and
shadow. He manipulated light through colour, which came from small
glass squares and motifs inset in doors and in free-standing uprights.
Colour became masculine and feminine, and he used both artificial and
natural light to achieve some of his most spectacular effects. Leaded
glass allowed him to carry a symbol from room to room, and his glass
designs were some of the most elegant and unusual features of his interiors.

Mackintosh, in the spirit of his Celtic forebears, employed the
use of metal in a variety of ways and he enjoyed the juxtaposition of

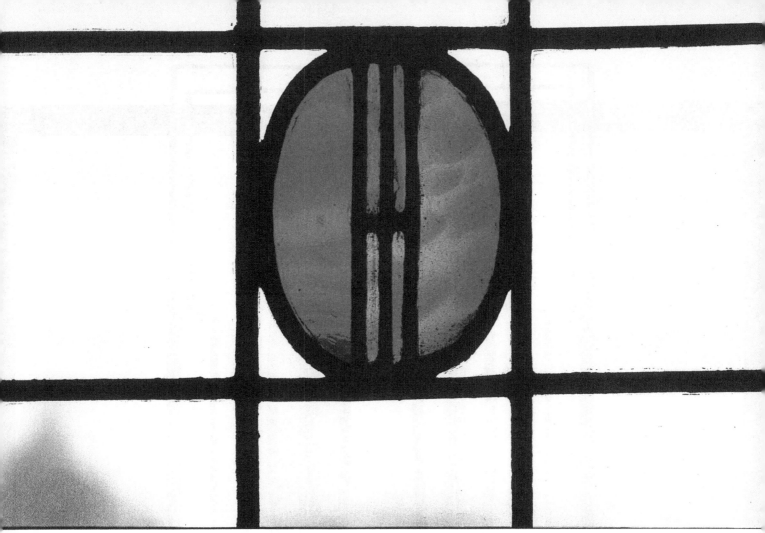

natural wood and stone against the modernity of metals. In his early career, his metalwork was functional and based on the drawings he made as he travelled across Britain and Italy. Mackintosh's simple metal handles, locks, hinges and braces were soon replaced by technically brilliant repoussé panels and beaten, punctured surfaces. He allowed metal beams to be exposed in his architectural works, and produced brackets and railings that both carried through a theme or motif, and invigorated simple design. He used metal to create natural and organic images, intertwining and knotting wrought iron to produce sturdy, yet completely fluid designs. He worked metal around and through glass to create yet another contrast between the impenetrable and the translucent.

Mackintosh used fabric as another means of employing both contrast and continuity. Plain muslin could both delineate a room and light it; it could produce a false, nearly sheer ceiling, or wrap windows with only the barest of coverings. He used embroidery and stencilling on fabric to create a unified symbolism within his interiors, featuring motifs that would appear both outside and inside a space, linking rooms with one another, and linking elements within a room. Margaret

Glass Detail from the Glasgow School of Art.

Mackintosh used glass to enhance many of his designs. He inset it in panels in his furniture, or used it to cast a coloured glow from his light fittings, and details in his doors, panels and windows.

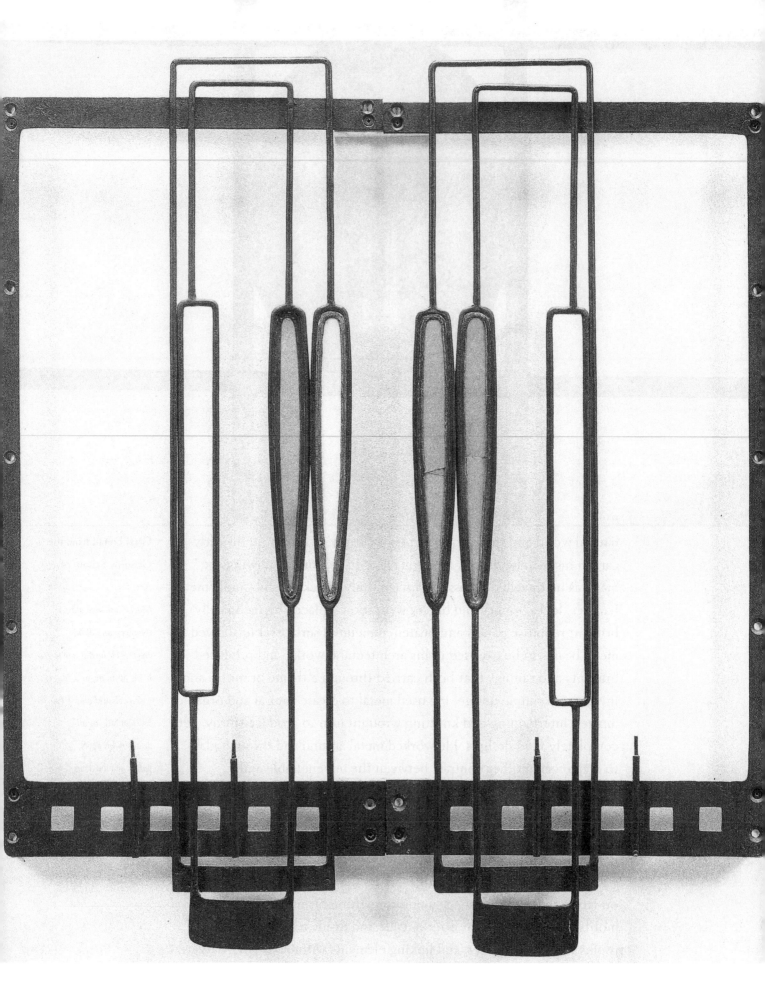

worked closely with Mackintosh in his use of fabric in design, and she created an engaging and romanticized femininity in textiles. Most of Mackintosh's Glasgow work involved textile designs for specific interiors, and these were normally hand-made in a laborious process.

Shortly after moving to London in 1915, Mackintosh received his first commercial commission for textile designs intended for mass production. Once again, his work reflects a dependence on organic forms, with boldly coloured, stylized flowers forming the most part of his design. He used repetition carelessly to enhance the vibrancy of the image, but also to stress its two-dimensionality. Ironically, he chose to adopt a feature of the Arts and Crafts Movement from which he had been dissociated, that of truth to the material, and for the first time in his decorative career, the overall art of the product seemed to come second to its function.

Margaret also worked as a freelance textile designer, and both the Mackintoshes were hired by two leading textile firms, Foxton's and Sefton's. While his earlier work reflects his preoccupation with nature, which still bound him after his furniture and architectural designs moved away from organic imagery, his later work is more geometric, with a bold use of

WHERE NATURAL IMAGES WERE USED, THEY BECAME HEAVILY STYLIZED AND ABSTRACT

colour and shape that anticipated Art Deco. Where natural images were used, they became heavily stylized and abstract.

The fabric designs were often created from elements in the Mackintoshes' paintings; in particular, *Blue and Pink Tobacco Flowers* recalls a detail from Margaret's *The Opera of the Sea*. They became skilled at producing harmonious designs based on crowded, repetitive motifs, and these represent the embodiment of Mackintosh's skill at using line and colour to overwhelming effect.

Like William Morris before him, Mackintosh was extremely versatile, adapting his style to suit various mediums, and creating unique works that quickly became distinguishing trademarks. For all his successes, Mackintosh was, however, disillusioned and frustrated by his inability to translate these various achievements into a school of art and architecture. He felt he had made little impact on Scotland, and even his European recognition was clouded by what most people considered to be a hazy and impossible vision. He had proved that he

Railing from the Willow Tea Rooms.
A section of railing made from wrought iron and leaded glass. Metal was one of Mackintosh's favourite mediums through which to create organic images such as this willow pattern.

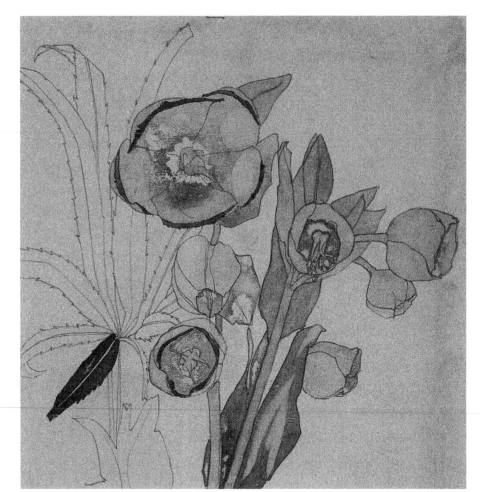

Helebore Green,
Watercolour.

The pantheistic element visible in this unfinished watercolour was inherent in Mackintosh's decorative work on Kate Cranston's tea rooms. The soft colours employed here were those used most often in the early part of his career.

could turn his hand to fine and applied arts as well as to architecture; he was the forerunner of the Glasgow Style and he had designed some of the most important buildings in Glasgow. But for Mackintosh this was not enough. His frustration turned to depression, and as he neared the end of his working life, he realized that his dream would not become a reality.

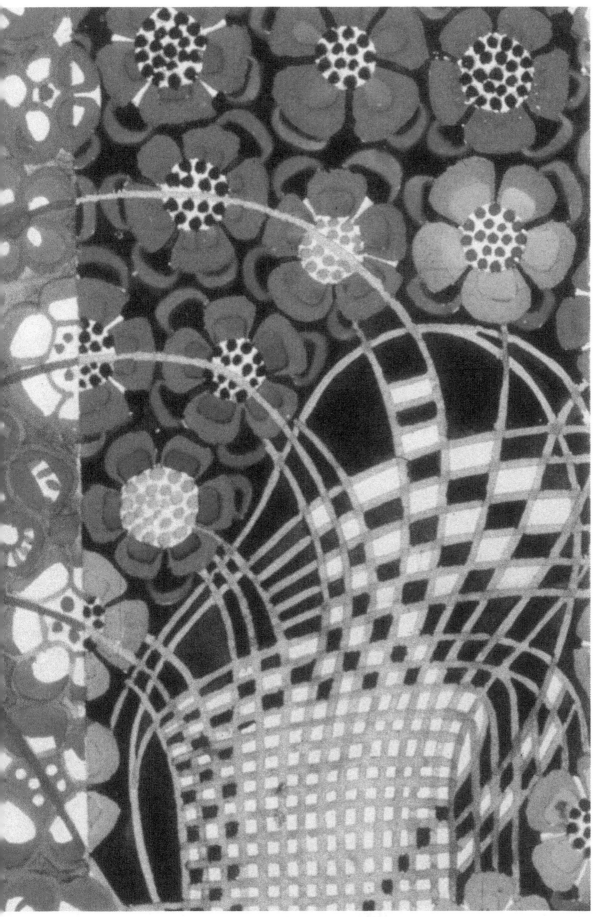

Blue and Pink Tobacco Flowers.

After moving to London, the Mackintoshes began to work on textile designs. They continued to favour images of nature, but these were now very stylized and often contrasted with areas of bold geometric shapes.

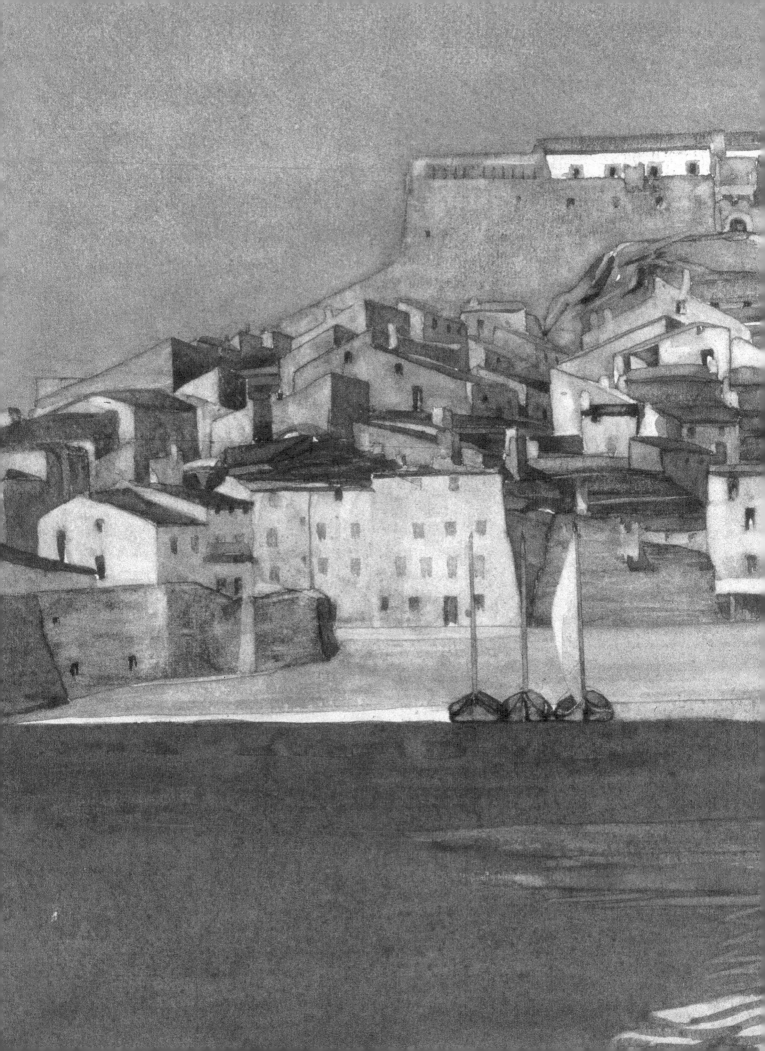

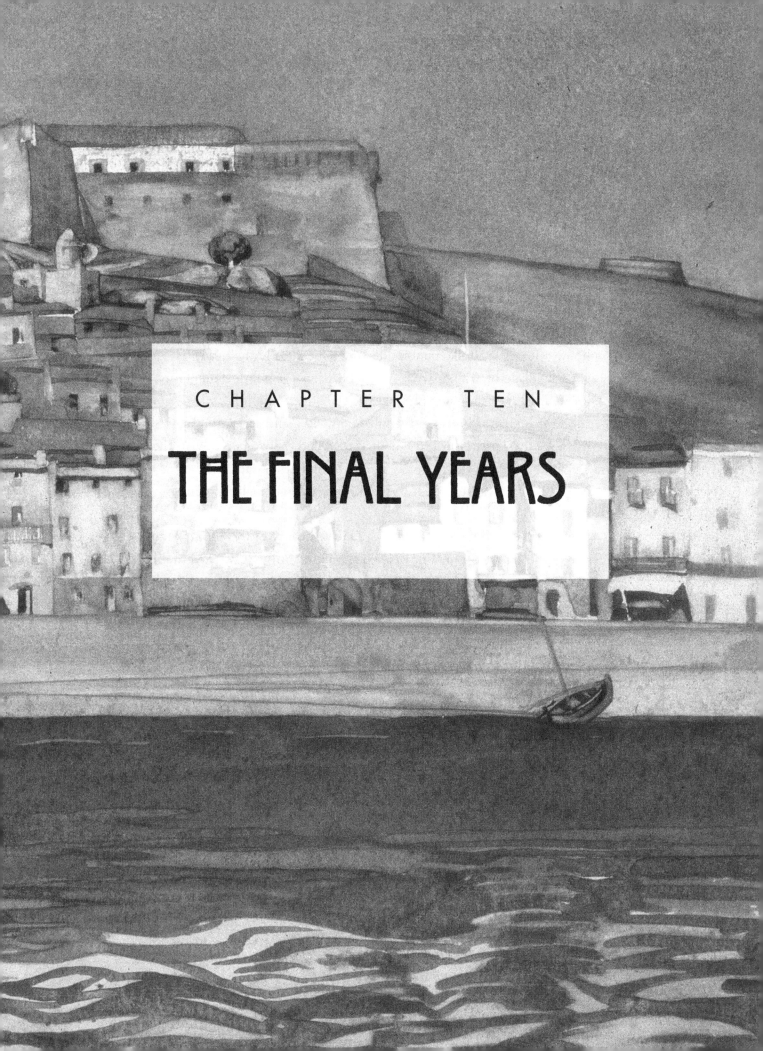

CHAPTER TEN

THE FINAL YEARS

If one were to go through the lists of truly original artists, the creative minds of the modern movement, the name of Charles Ronnie Mackintosh would certainly be included even amongst the few that one can count on the fingers of a single hand.

Hermann Muthesius (1861–1927)

AFTER LEAVING Glasgow, the Mackintoshes never returned. Charles' envisioned school had never materialized, and he had, tor the most part, shared the credit for his work with his colleagues. Ties were severed with Keppie, who had never really forgiven him for jilting his sister, but who did, nonetheless, treat Mackintosh fairly when their partnership was dissolved.

Margaret and Charles left Glasgow – closing but not selling their home – for the Suffolk countryside, more specifically the beautiful coastal village of Walberswick. Walberswick was a gentle community, located south of the River Blyth at the top edge of Suffolk. Mackintosh had first visited the village in 1897, and soon after his marriage to Margaret in 1900, he had travelled there again to visit the Newbery family at their holiday home. Initially the Mackintoshes rented a flat at Millside, next to the Newberys, eventually moving on to Westwood on Lodge Road.

Mackintosh took great pleasure in the beauty of the countryside, and in the proliferation of flowers and other plantlife. It was a veritable haven for a nature-lover, and the fens were covered with flowering plants: sea milkwort, slender trefoil, sea lavender and clurs rushes. Their Westwood home had once been surrounded by a thousand trees, and the landscape was dotted with hedgerows, wood anemone, betony and laurel.

Mackintosh found great comfort in this natural world, and painted for long hours each day, sitting in his glorious garden and taking time to contemplate and study in the peaceful seclusion of his home. There is a sense of freedom in his works from Walberswick which was not found in his work either before or after this period. In 1902, Mackintosh had stated, 'Art is the flower – life is the green leaf. Let every artist strive to make his flower a beautiful living thing, something that will convince the world that there may be; that there are things more precious, more beautiful, more lasting than life. But to do this you must offer real, living, beautifully coloured flowers, flowers that grow but from above the green leaf; flowers that are not dead; are not dying; not artificial; real flowers springing from your own soul – not

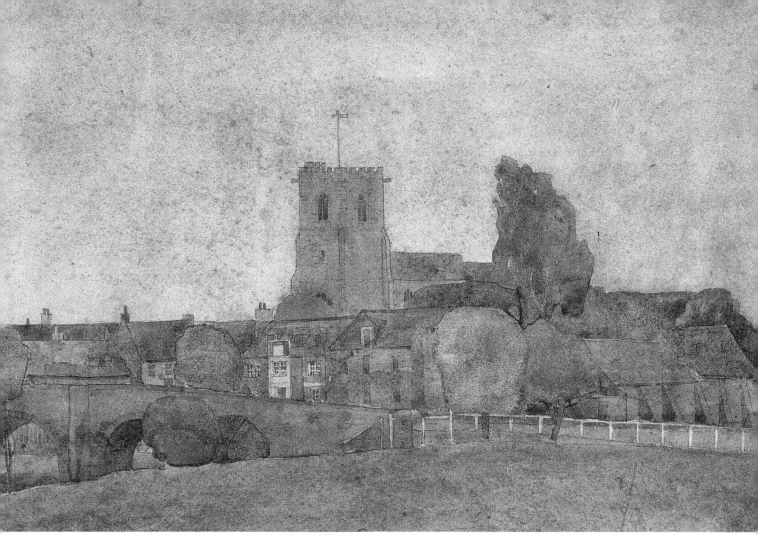

even cut flowers – you must offer the flowers of the art that is in you – the symbols of all that is noble – and beautiful – and inspiring – flowers that will often change a colourless cheerless life into an animated thoughtfulness.' These words were to become prophecy, for although Mackintosh had at this time no real aspirations to give up architecture and his trampled philosophy, his interests had shifted and he now, perhaps instinctively, took the time to find animation in a life that had become blackened by despair.

He concentrated on a series of flower and plant studies that worked their way from being accurate botanical subjects to abstract and more stylized images. He experimented with colour and form, and produced an exquisite collection of watercolours that exemplify his changing spirit. He had one architectural commission during these early years of exile, at 78 Derngate, and a number of unfulfilled projects, and eventually, in 1915, the Mackintoshes moved to London.

The next eight years marked a period of rebirth, and they became known as the 'Chelsea Years'. Kate Cranston contacted him once again in 1917 to design 'The Dug-Out', a basement addition to the Willow Tea Rooms, and characteristically Mackintosh rose to the

Wareham in Dorset.

Mackintosh's watercolours reflected the comfort he found in the beauty of the countryside. During his lifetime, he made many trips to the West Country where he filled several sketchbooks with his drawings. Few, however, became finished watercolours.

Settle from the Dug Out.

The Dug Out was an addition to the Willow Tea Rooms. As this was in the basement, he alleviated the darkness with bright yellow settles and stencilled designs in blue and green

challenge and produced a holistic design incorporating furniture, screens, stencils, carpeting and a splendid mural carrying through a chevron motif.

The war had called a halt to most major building work, and Mackintosh struggled to set up a private architectural practice. When money began to dry up, the couple began their textile design work, which was purchased by Foxton's and Sefton's in Belfast, and by Liberty in London. Their designs were exciting and unique, characterized by a daring use of colour, working through organic designs to bold geometric shapes. Mackintosh also produced a number of watercolours, which he sold to increase their income, often calling upon former patrons, such as William Davidson of Windyhill, to help out.

Although times were hard financially, this was a period of great cultural fulfilment for the Mackintoshes. They became involved with a number of local projects, including the London Salon of the Independents, which sponsored 'open' exhibitions, and The Plough, a theatre group for whom they designed sets and costumes. They also became friendly with George Bernard Shaw, the composer Eugene Goosens, the dancer Margaret Morris, and the painter J. D. Ferguson, among others, and despite their difficulties, they seemed content.

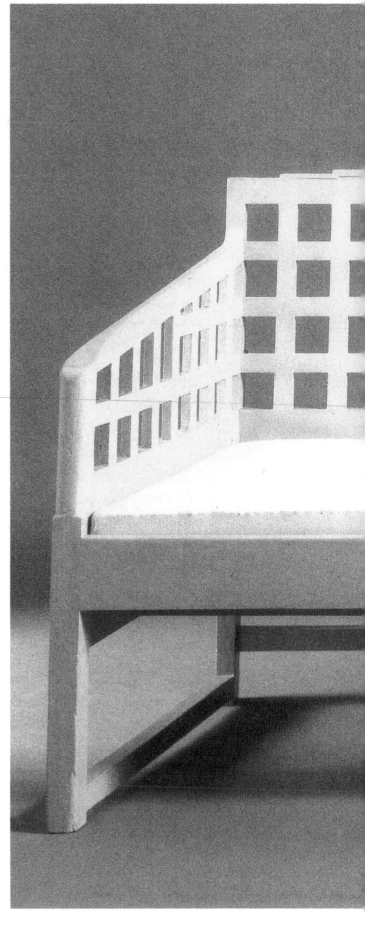

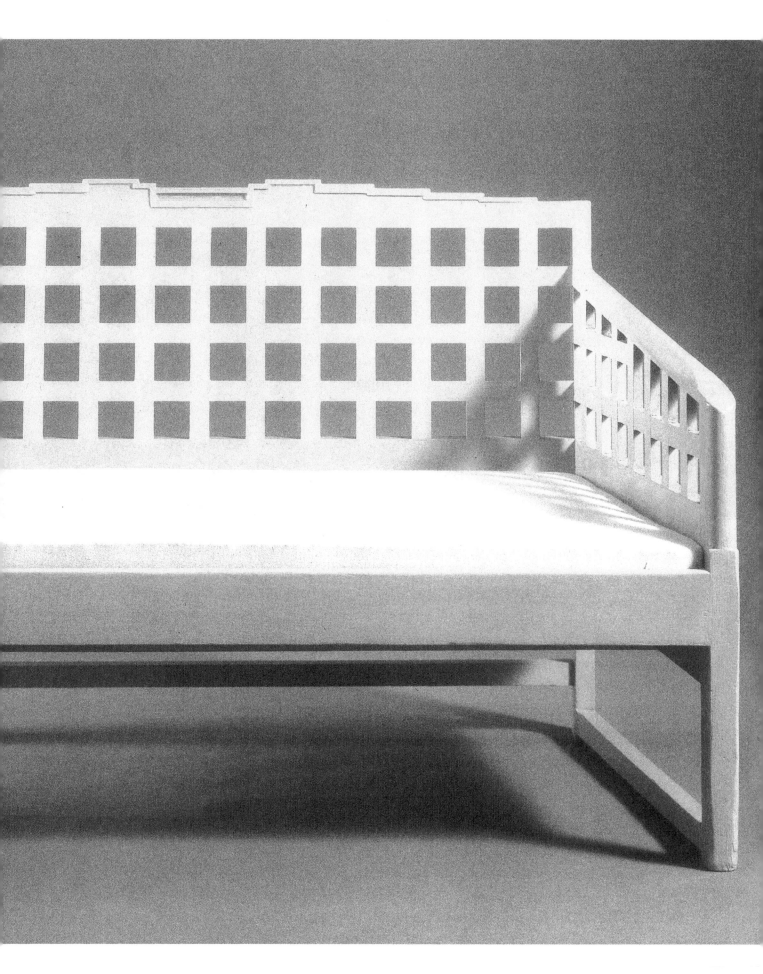

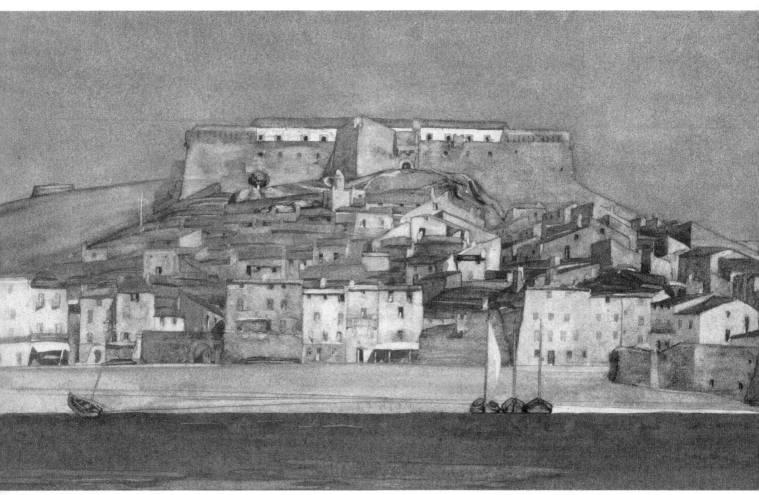

Coullioure.

Once the Mackintoshes had settled in the South of France, Charles took up his watercolours once again, making studies of flowers and plants and painting landscapes.

In 1920, Mackintosh was offered two commissions – one for a studio house for the painter Harold Squire, another for a block of studio flats for the Arts League of Service, and later, a small theatre for Margaret Morris. Sadly, none of these commissions reached fruition, and he was unable to find a suitable patron in London circles. Finally, they were forced to sell their Glasgow home, and in 1923 the Mackintoshes left Britain for the South of France.

Originally, the intention was to have a long holiday in the sun and to recover from the dispiriting latter years in London, but they settled at Port Vendres, on the Mediterranean side of the French-Spanish border and stayed there for four years. Mackintosh had finally given up on his architectural aspirations, and with characteristic spirit and optimism, set himself the task of perfecting his watercolours. His work was comprised of atmospheric, evocative landscapes, and colourful studies of flowers and plants. Ironically, these paintings represent a perfect expression of decorative form and the use of line, for although Mackintosh had made a conscious decision to move away from architecture, he was unable to do so on a spiritual level, and his work represented yet another level of his architectural vision.

The landscapes are colourful and assertive, and illustrate once again Mackintosh's profound respect for nature. Roger Billcliffe wrote: 'Mackintosh did not set out to capture movement. It is a concept that he avoids, even in his flower drawings, for their petals are unruffled by the wind, their stems unswaying; and in the views of Port Vendres, the ripples of water in the bay are frozen into a static diagram ... his concentration was fixed on the immovable and permanent.'

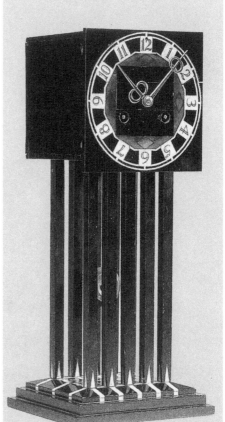

Ebonised Clock.
This clock was made in around 1917. Its bold, unusual design, with contrasts of black and white and inlaid decoration is typically Mackintosh.

He painted for long hours, spending sometimes weeks on one painting. His perfectionist instincts had not dulled, and he found a new vehicle for his sharp mind and need for expression. He was, however, ill-paid for his work, and an exhibition set up at the Leicester Galleries in London failed to raise sufficient funds to call his new work a living. However Margaret and Mackintosh remembered these years as the best in their lives, and they shared a quiet intimacy that was both intense and essential to their happiness together. Margaret returned to London periodically for decorative commissions, and Mackintosh wrote to her faithfully, his letters warm and whimsical, full of his thoughts for her and for their life together.

In the autumn of 1927, Mackintosh returned to England, having suffered a serious illness which was finally diagnosed as cancer of the tongue. He was unable to speak, and became invalided in a London hospital, where he was taught sign-language by the ever-engaging Margaret Morris. He died, at the age of 60, on 19 December 1928, and was cremated at Golders Green Cemetery after a quiet ceremony.

Margaret Mackintosh died four years later in London. Her estate was valued at only £88, 16 shillings and two pence.

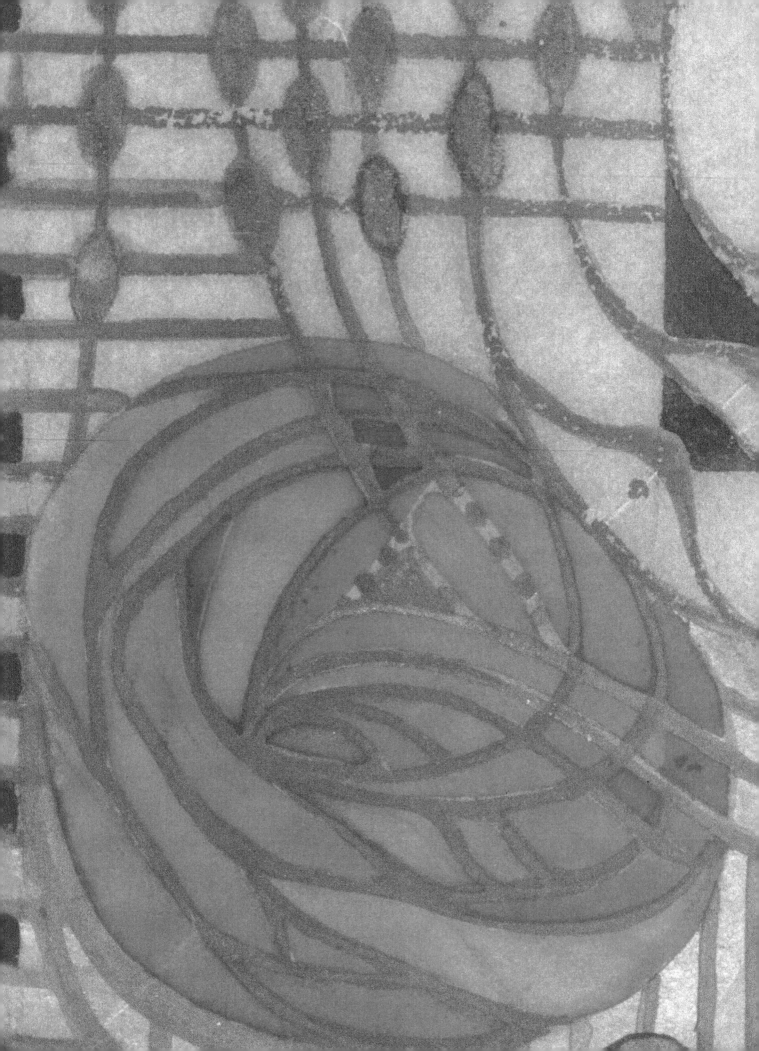

AFTER MACKINTOSH

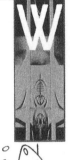

WHEN MACKINTOSH moved to Port Vendres, he retreated in both
body and spirit. There was the occasional spark of interest in his work,
but he refused to take part in any critical study, harbouring a resent-
ment and perhaps anxiety about the world he had relinquished. In
1924, Charles Marriot, the architecture critic of *The Times*, wrote a piece
entitled Modern English Architecture, in which he said, 'It is hardly
too much to say that the whole modernist movement in European
architecture derives from him'. Mackintosh was asked to contribute his
views to various architectural journals, but he abruptly refused, alienat-
ed from the culture he had left behind and scathing about the lack of
soul and purpose in his contemporaries.

When he died, Margaret tried unsuccessfully to organize an
exhibition of Mackintosh's work, but four months after her own death,
the drawings, watercolours and furniture that remained were brought
together to form a Memorial Exhibition in Glasgow. The exhibition
offered him some long-awaited acclaim, but there was no comprehensive understanding of his work, and little interest in uncovering one. The
contents of Hous'hill were auctioned – at low prices – but Mackintosh
was of little importance in his home city, and his work was largely
considered to be outdated.

A whisper of new interest came from the architects of the new
Modernism, who claimed that Mackintosh was their pioneer and that
with startling genius he had anticipated their essential vision many
years before its inception. This small group of enthusiastic journalists
and architects struggled to establish Charles Rennie Mackintosh's place
in history, but their contemporaries were uninterested. He was associ-
ated, incorrectly, with an Art Nouveau designer, and called the father
of Art Deco by some, but perhaps the most important point was that
Mackintosh did not set out to follow or to create any stylistic movement.
He worked outside everything contemporary, struggling to assert his
own individuality and high standards.

Some critics have suggested that his reconciliation of the capacity
of science with the needs of the individual – or the soul – mirrored the
nineteenth century metaphysical philosophy of Hegelianism. Certainly

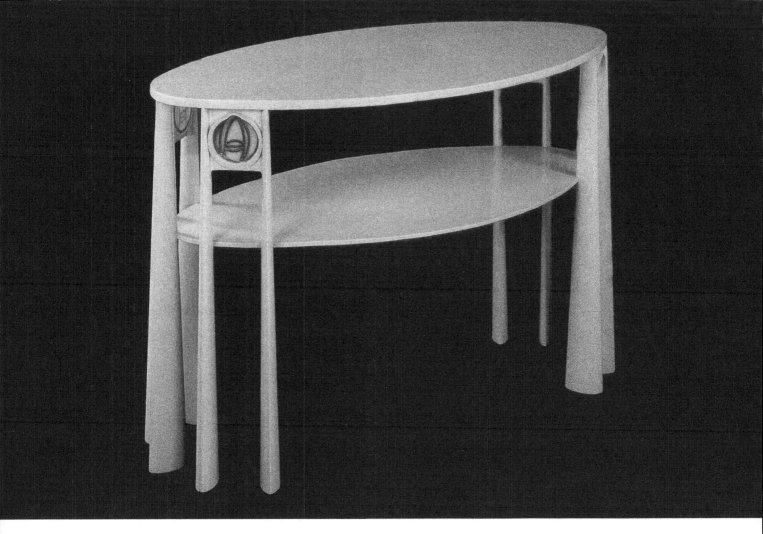

his commitment to holistic design and total organic unity confirms this view, but his work had a much broader spectrum, and the ideology behind it was unique and ever-changing. For this reason, he could never have had a school of followers, nor could he have had a wide-ranging influence on other artists and architects.His highly individualist vision was unique, and he was unable to create a justifiable and sustainable dogma to explain his work. Like Lethaby, he believed in humanism, and he opposed the Modern Movement's obsession with technology. But he was undoubtedly one of the precursors to organic Modernism and it was his own dogged determination to create on his own terms that prevented his work from becoming universally accepted and ultimately influential.

In *Pioneers of the Modern Movement*, Pevsner wrote: 'In order to understand Mackintosh, it is essential to grasp the fusion in his art of puritanism with sensuality. The enchanting curves of Art Nouveau have the same importance as the austere verticals of the incipient Modern Movement.' It was this blend of styles that was Mackintosh's own interpretation of what was around him, combined with his own distinct view of what and how he wanted to create, that made him

Oval Table.

This lacquered oval table was possibly made in 1903 for the exhibition in Moscow. It has the leaded glass insets that Mackintosh favoured at this time, in the familiar rose motif.

unique. His work has appeared in later exhibitions of Art Nouveau, and indeed formed the largest single exhibit in the Parisian Les Sources du XXe Siècle: Les Arts en Europe de 1884–1914, in 1960–61. Alan Crawford believes that Art Nouveau was a more appropriate context for his work than Modernism, writing that 'Though Mackintosh's straight lines made as little sense alongside the rich curves of French and Belgian Art Nouveau, as did those of the Viennese, this context made more historical sense of him than Modernism had. His decorative work could now be understood alongside the structural, and in his own time. In the growing enthusiasm for Art Nouveau in the 1960s, Mackintosh found a prominent place.'

The interest in Mackintosh's work following his death did lead to collections of his work being formed, in particular, at the Glasgow School of Art and the Hunterian Art Gallery of the University of Glasgow in the 1940s. Many of the original furniture and fittings are in use in the Glasgow School of Art, and the 'Mackintosh Room', which was the original boardroom, houses an important collection of his drawings and watercolours, while the Furniture Gallery of the School displays his furnishings.

HIS DECORATIVE WORK COULD NOW BE UNDERSTOOD ALONGSIDE THE STRUCTURAL

The Ingram Street Tea Rooms were dismantled in 1971, and purchased by the Glasgow City Art Gallery and Museum at Kelvingrove, and a reconstructed section of the Chinese Room is now on view. In the late 1970s, the Charles Rennie Mackintosh Society was founded at Queen's Cross Church. Hill House was passed into the hands of the National Trust for Scotland, and most of it is now open to the public, while undergoing restoration work. Even the structure of the Willow Tea Rooms, which were remodelled by the department store which had last occupied it, have been carefully reinstated, and the building now retains much of its individual flavour and appearance. The Hunterian Art Gallery houses the Southpark Avenue interiors, and a new extension has the contents of Mackintosh's home on view.

Design for a Printed Textile. Although Mackintosh is best remembered for architecture, it was his exquisitely original work in textiles, glass, furniture and furnishings which first brought him recognition.

In the 1970s, Mackintosh became big business, with a single chair going for £9300 at auction. Reproduction Mackintosh furniture was produced, particularly by Cassina of Milan. Even Letraset produced a collection of Mackintosh lettering, which has become one of the most popular decorative typefaces available.

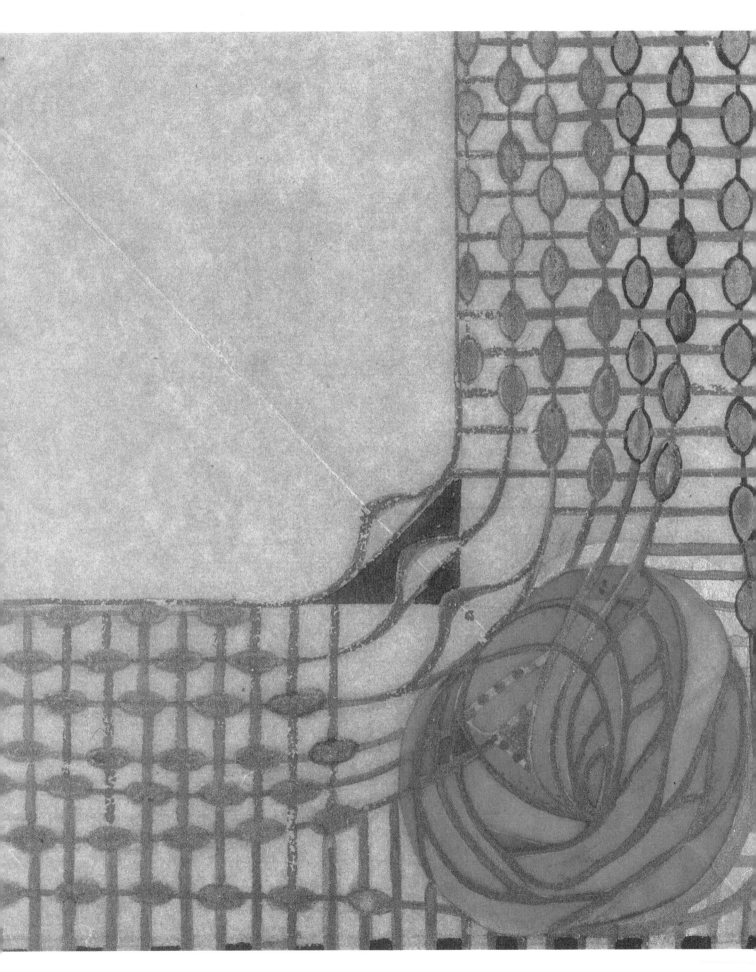

AFTER MACKINTOSH

119

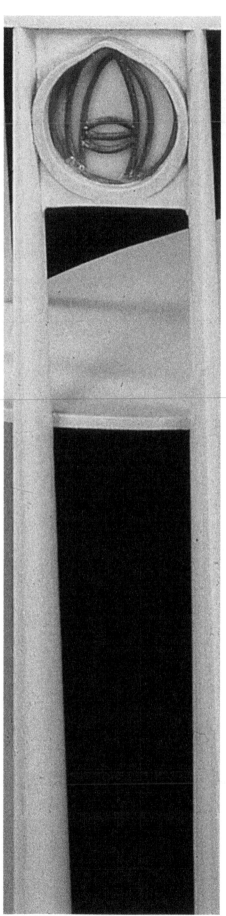

Detail from Oval Table.

The repetitive use of symbolism and motifs across the range of his work, not only provided a unity to Mackintosh's collections, but also enhanced the environment for which they were created.

Many academics have attempted to discover the root of his style, and to attribute schools of art to its conception; similarly, his influence has been broadly defined, but never pinpointed. In 1983, the Mackintosh Society organized a conference entitled 'Mackintosh: National and International', with papers on Muthesius, Frank Lloyd Wright, Greene and Greene, Gaudi and others. Alan Crawford writes that 'The idea behind the conference was that Mackintosh was one of a handful of architects and designers in Europe and America at the turn of the century who drew inspiration for their modernism from national or regional vernaculars; and that there may have been something like an international style before the Bauhaus, with Mackintosh as its catalyst .... Like Modernism, it gives Mackintosh heroic status, and like the 1960s enthusiasm for Art Nouveau, it allows his work to be seen as a whole and in its own time.'

Crawford maintains that his work did not look forward to Modernism, although it is easy to see why the Modernists looked back to him. He claims that Mackintosh was an ordinary, hardworking and talented man, but that he did not always know where he was going. Hence the diversity of his work, and the dramatic change in style he was able to create. The extraordinary difference between Mains Street, and the Glasgow School of Art, between Hill Mouse and Derngate, between Queen's Cross Church and the tea rooms, shows an artist of wide-ranging vision, one who was able to create a space and fill it according to the needs of the occupants. It is organic, holistic, individualist design created by an individual for the individual, and therefore everything he did was unique. There was a liberal and repetitive use of symbolism and motifs across his work, which provides a unity to his collections, but those motifs and symbols work within their environment and stand alone, compelling the observer to examine their inter-relation but speaking a different language to everyone who viewed them.

Mackintosh's creations worked within and outside their environment; they are a perfectly integrated whole, and unique pieces characterized by breath-taking originality. The American critic Ada Louise Huxtable wrote: 'The chairs of Charles Rennie Mackintosh are spectral. They are presences. They upstage people. They have more strength and identity than anyone in the room'.

Mackintosh was a profound transformer. He integrated the Scottish vernacular, the English Free Style, the Viennese use of line and space, the organic imagery that was the product of his passion for nature, the Glasgow Style and the extraordinarily original and spiritual vision of his combined efforts with Margaret into one intellectual entity that was uniquely his. And even then, he had the remarkable ability to change, to plunder the seemingly unfathomable depths of his imagination for new and more exciting designs. Mackintosh's importance lay in his ability to design and to create what he did, not in his place in the broader scheme of things, and for that reason he will stand alone. The original genius.

CHRONOLOGY

1864   Margaret Macdonald born in the English Midlands.

1868   Charles Rennie Mackintosh born in Glasgow, on 7 June. Parents: William McIntosh and Margaret Rennie McIntosh.

1874   McIntosh family move to 2 Firpark Terrace, Dennistoun.

1884   Mackintosh begins apprenticeship with John Hutchison, and enrols as a part-time student at the Glasgow School of Art.

1885   Mackintosh's mother dies.

1889   Joins architectural studio of Honeyman and Keppie, and continues at the School of Art. Wins Queen's Prize at South Kensington, and the Design Prize at Glasgow Institute.

1890   Wins the Alexander Thomson Travelling Scholarship for design for *A Public Hall*. Designs *Redclyffe House*.

1891   Presents 'Scotch Baronial Architecture' lecture to Glasgow Architecural Association.

1891   Tours Italy, London and Paris.

1891   Frances and Margaret Macdonald enrol at Glasgow School of Art.

1892   Wins gold medal for *A Chapter House* in the Soane Medallion Competition.

1893   Probably the year in which Charles changed his name from McIntosh to Mackintosh.

1894   Designs hall and library at Craigie Hall. Undertakes drawings for Queen Margaret's Medical College.

1895   Produces interior designs at Gladmuir, for the Davidsons, and for Lennox Castle Inn, Lennoxtown.

1896   Draws poster for *The Scottish Music Review*. The Four exhibit at the London Arts and Crafts Society – hostile reviews. Interior work at Buchanan Street Tea Rooms with George Walton, commissioned by Kate Cranston.

1897   Construction of first phase of the Glasgow School of Art. Produces furniture for the Argyle Street Tea Rooms. Work featured in *The Studio* magazine.

1898   Produces drawings for the 1901 Glasgow Exhibition. Work appears in *Dekorative Kunst* magazine. Commissioned by Bruchmann to produce dining room in Munich.

1899   Designs for Windyhill commissioned by William Davidson.

1900   Marries Margaret Macdonald. Produces interiors and furniture for

Dunglass Castle, Bowling for the Macdonalds. Interiors at the Ingram Street Tea Rooms. The Four invited to exhibit at the eighth Secession Exhibition in Vienna. Travels to Vienna with Margaret.

1901 Windyhill completed. Designs exhibition stands for the International Exhibition. Interiors of 14 Kinsborough Gardens, Glasgow commissioned by Mrs Roaat. Provides additions to the Ingram Street Tea Rooms.

1902 Travels to Italy. Exhibits at the International Exhibition of Modern Decorative Art, Turin. Drawings for Liverpool Cathedral competition.

1903 Drawings for Hill House, Helensburgh, commissioned by Walter Blackie. Designs the Willow Tea Rooms.

1904 Hill House under construction. Interiors for Holy Trinity Church. Willow Tea Rooms opens. Mackintosh made partner in the firm of Honeyman and Keppie.

1905 Designs more furnishings for Hill House, the Tea Rooms, Windyhill and Hous'hill.

1906 The Mackintoshes move to 78 Southpark Avenue. Produces designs for the west wing of the School of Art, Mosside, Kilmacolm, The Oak Room at Ingram Street Tea Rooms and The Dutch Kitchen at Argyle Street Tea Rooms.

1907 Construction of west wing of the School of Art begins. Doorway to the Lady Artists Club, Glasgow. Travels to Portugal.

1908 Designs interiors at Hous'hill, and The Oval Room and interiors at the Ingram Street Tea Rooms.

1911 Creates the Cloister Room and The Chinese Room at Ingram Street Tea Rooms. The White Cockade restaurant at the Glasgow Exhibition.

1913 Leaves Honeyman, Keppie and Mackintosh.

1914 Leaves Glasgow for Walberswick, England. Studies flowers and plant life.

1915 Moves to Chelsea. Begins fabric designs for Foxton's and Sefton's.

1917 Bedroom for S. Horstman, Bath. The Dug Out and The Willow Tea Rooms, Glasgow.

1918 Sells Glasgow house to William Davidson. Designs striped bedroom for W. J. Bassett-Lowke.

1920 Furniture and interiors for Bassett-Lowke, theatre designs and book commissions.

1923 Moves to Port Vendres France, and begins watercolour studies.

1927 Returns to London. Suffers from cancer of the tongue.

1928 Charles Rennie Mackintosh dies.

1933 Margaret Macdonald Mackintosh dies.

FURTHER READING

Architecture, Design & Works of Art

Billcliffe, Roger, *Architectural Sketches & Flower Drawings by Charles Rennie Mackintosh*, Academy Editions, London, 1977.

Billcliffe, Roger, *Charles Rennie Mackintosh: The Complete Furniture, Furniture Drawings and Interior Designs*, John Murray Publishers Ltd., London, 1986.

Billcliffe, Roger, *Mackintosh Watercolours*, John Murray Publishers Ltd., London, 1978.

Billcliffe, Roger, *Mackintosh Textile Designs*, The Fine Arts Society/John Murray Publishers Ltd., London, 1982.

Buchanan, William, *Mackintosh's Masterwork: the Glasgow School of Art*, Drew, Glasgow, 1989.

Cooper, Jackie, *Mackintosh Architecture: the Complete Buildings & Selected Projects*, Academy Editions, London, 1984.

Filippo, Alison, *Charles Rennie Mackintosh as a Designer of Chairs*, (trans. Bruno & Cristina Del Priore), Warehouse Publications, London, 1974.

Grigor, Murray, *The Architect's Architect: Charles Rennie Mackintosh*, Bellew Publishing, London, 1993.

Macaulay, James, *Glasgow School Of Art: Charles Rennie Mackintosh*, Phaidon, London, 1993.

Macleod, Robert, *Charles Rennie Mackintosh: Architect and Artist*, Collins & Son, Glasgow, 1983.

Robertson, Pamela, ed., *Architectural Papers by Charles Rennie Mackintosh*, White Cockade in association with the Hunterian Art Gallery, Glasgow, 1990.

Robertson, Pamela. *C. R. Mackintosh: the chelsea Years 1915–1923*, Hunterian Art Gallery, Glasgow, 1994.

Biography

Crawford, Alan, *Charles Rennie Mackintosh*, Thames and Hudson, London, 1995.

Fiell, Charlotte, *Charles Rennie Mackintosh (1868–1928)*, Taschen, London, 1995.

Grigg, Jocelyn, *Charles Rennie Mackintosh*, Drew, Glasgow, 1987.

Hackney, Fiona, *Charles Rennie Mackintosh*, Grange Books, London, 1996.

Helland, Janice, *The Studios of Frances & Margaret Macdonald*, Manchester University Press, Manchester, 1996.

Jones, Anthony, *Charles Rennie Mackintosh*, Studio Editions, London 1994.

Kaplan, Wendy, *Charles Rennie Mackintosh*, Abbeville Press, London, 1996.

Moffat, Alistair & Baxter, Colin, *Remembering Charles Rennie Mackintosh*, Lanark & Colin Baxter Photography, 1989.

Criticism and Interpretation

Steele, James, *Synthesis in Form*, Academy Editions, London, 1994.

Wilhide, Elizabeth, *The Mackintosh Style: Decor & Design*, Pavilion Books, London, 1995.

Howarth, Thomas, *Charles Rennie Mackintosh & the Modern Movement*, Routledge and Keegan Paul, London, 1952.

Neat, Timothy, *Part Seen, Part Imagined: Meaning & Symbolism in the Work of Charles Rennie Mackintosh & Margaret Macdonald*, Canongate Press, London, 1994.

Nuttgens, Patrick, ed., *Mackintosh and his Contemporaries in Europe and America*, John Murray Publishers Ltd., London, 1988.

Pevsner, Nikolaus, *Pioneers of Modern Design*, Penguin Books, London, 1984.

Robertson, Pamela, *Charles Rennie Mackintosh: Art is the Flower*, Pavilion Books, 1995.

PICTURE CREDITS

Page 6 Detail from The Wassail. Courtesy of Christie's Images. **Pages 8-9** Sheet of Studies of Mosaic Bands, Orvieto Cathedral. Courtesy of Christie's Images. **Page 11** Glass Detail from Hill House. Courtesy of Anthony Oliver. **Page 12** The Garden at Hill House. Courtesy of The Bridgeman Art Library. **Page 15** Flower Study – Mont Louis. Courtesy of Christie's Images. **Page 16** Study of a Statue of St Jerome (Recto), Milan Cathedral. Courtesy of Christie's Images. **Pages 18 & 19** Detail from Sheet of Studies of Mosaic Bands, Orvieto Cathedral. Courtesy of Christie's Images. **Pages 20-1** Detail of Wall Stencil in Drawing Room at Hill House. Courtesy of the National Trust for Scotland. **Page 23** Design for an Exhibition Stand. Courtesy of Christie's Images. **Pages 24 & 25** A Metal and Leaded Glass Hanging Shade. Courtesy of Christie's Images. **Page 27** A Metal and Leaded Glass Hanging Shade. Courtesy of Christie's Images. **Page 29** Detail of Wall Stencil in Drawing Room at Hill House. Courtesy of the National Trust for Scotland. **Pages 30 & 31** A Mahogany Washstand. Courtesy of Christie's Images. **Page 33** Floral and Chequered Fabric Design. Courtesy of Christie's Images. **Pages 34-5** Board Room in the Glasgow School of Art. Courtesy of Anthony Oliver. **Page 37** Main Entrance of the Glasgow School of Art. Courtesy of Anthony Oliver. **Page 38** Glasgow School of Art: A Studio. Courtesy of The Bridgeman Art Library. **Page 39** Detail from Studies of the Ceiling Decoration of the Certosa di Pavia. Courtesy of Christie's Images. **Page 41** Studies of the Ceiling Decoration of the Certosa di Pavia. Courtesy of Christie's Images. **Page 43** Western Elevation of the Glasgow School of Art. Courtesy of Anthony Oliver. **Page 44** Board Room in the Glasgow School of Art. Courtesy of Anthony Oliver. **Page 47** Library in the Glasgow School of Art. Courtesy of Anthony Oliver. **Pages 48-9** Main Bedroom in Hill House. Courtesy of Anthony Oliver. **Page 51** Detail from Main Bedroom in Hill House. Courtesy of Anthony Oliver. **Pages 52-3** Still Life of Anemones. Courtesy of The Bridgeman Art Library. **Page 54** Still Life of Anemones. Courtesy of The Bridgeman Art Library. **Pages 56-7** Interior of the Queen's Cross Chruch. Courtesy of Anthony Oliver. **Page 59** Dining Room Designed for the Art Lover's House. Courtesy of The Bridgeman Art Library. **Page 60** Apple, Walberswick. Courtesy of The Bridgeman Art Library. **Page 63** Interior of the Queen's Cross Chruch. Courtesy of Anthony Oliver. **Pages 64-5** The Wassail. Courtesy of Christie's Images. **Page 66** Detail from The Wassail. Courtesy of Christie's Images. **Page 68** Detail from The Wassail. Courtesy of Christie's Images. **Pages 68 & 69** Cabinet with Painted Decoration. Courtesy of The Bridgeman Art Library. **Pages 70-1** View from the Garden of the Art Lover's House. Courtesy of Anthony Oliver. Pages **72 & 73** Writing Desk for Hill House. Courtesy of The Bridgeman Art Library. **Pages 74-5** Interior of the Stair Tower in the Scotland Street School. Courtesy of Anthony Oliver. **Page 77** Detail of the Beam above the Altar in the Queen's Cross Church. Courtesy of Anthony Oliver. **Page 79** North Elevation of Windyhill. Courtesy of Anthony Oliver. **Pages 80-1** View from the Garden of Hill House. Courtesy of Anthony Oliver. **Page 83** Drawing Room at Hill House. Courtesy of Anthony Oliver. **Page 84** Interior of the Stair Tower in the Scotland Street School. Courtesy of Anthony Oliver. **Pages 86-7** Detail of Glass Panel in the Willow Tearoom. Courtesy of Anthony Oliver. **Pages 88-9** Mural Decoration for the Buchanan Street Tea Room. Courtesy of The Bridgeman Art Library. **Page 90** Sign for the Willow Tearoom. Courtesy of Anthony Oliver. **Page 91** Detail of Glass Panel in the Willow Tearoom. Courtesy of Anthony Oliver. **Page 93** Bedroom at 78 Derngate. Courtesy of Anthony Oliver. **Page 94** Fireplace in the Drawing Room at Hill House. Courtesy of Anthony Oliver. **Page 95** Detail from Desk for the Blue Bedroom at Hous'hill. Courtesy of The Bridgeman Art Library. **Pages 96-7** Blue and Pink Tobacco Flowers. Courtesy of The Bridgeman Art Library. **Page 99** Ladderback Chair from Hill House. Courtesy of the National Trust for Scotland. **Page 100** Detail from Wardrobe in Hill House, Courtesy of the National Trust for Scotland. **Page 101** Glass Detail from the Glasgow School of Art. Courtesy of Anthony Oliver. **Page 102** Section of Wrought Iron and Leaded Glass Railing. Courtesy of Christie's Images. **Page 104** Helebore Green. Courtesy of Visual Arts Library. **Page 105** Blue and Pink Tobacco Flowers. Courtesy of The Bridgeman Art Library. **Pages 106-7** Collioure. Courtesy of The Bridgeman Art Library. **Page 109** Wareham, Dorset. Courtesy of Christie's Images. **Pages 110-11** Settle from Dug Out, Willow Tearoom. Courtesy of The Bridgeman Art Library. **Pages 112** Collioure. Courtesy of The Bridgeman Art Library. **Page 113** Ebonised Clock with Inlaid Decoration. Courtesy of The Bridgeman Art Library. **Pages 114-15** Design for a Printed Textile. Courtesy of The Bridgeman Art Library. **Page 117** Lacquered Oval Table with Leaded Glass Inserts. Courtesy of The Bridgeman Art Library. **Page 119** Design for a Printed Textile. Courtesy of The Bridgeman Art Library. **Page 120** Detail from Lacquered Oval Table with Leaded Glass Inserts. Courtesy of The Bridgeman Art Library.

INDEX

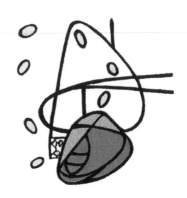

Lightning Source UK Ltd.
Milton Keynes UK
UKOW07f1350150216

268393UK00012B/71/P